Shelter, Nurture, and Spiritual Fellowship of the Children of God

Elizabeth F. Caldwell

Witherspoon Press
Louisville, Kentucky

Quotations from the *Book of Order* and *The Book of Confessions* of the Presbyterian Church (U.S.A.) are used with permission of the Office of the General Assembly of the Presbyterian Church (U.S.A.).

Unless otherwise noted, Scripture quotations are from the New Revised Standard Version of the Bible, copyright © 1989 by the Division of Christian Education of the National Council of the Churches of Christ in the U.S.A. Used by permission.

Book interior and cover design by Jeanne Williams

First edition

Published by Witherspoon Press
Louisville, Kentucky

Web site address: www.pcusa.org/witherspoonpress

PRINTED IN THE UNITED STATES OF AMERICA

06 07 08 09 10 11 12 13 14 15—10 9 8 7 6 5 4 3 2 1

Library of Congress Cataloging-in-Publication Data

Caldwell, Elizabeth, 1948-
  The shelter, nurture, and spiritual fellowship of the children of God
/Elizabeth F. Caldwell; Martha Gilliss, editor. -- 1st ed.
      p. cm.
    ISBN 1-57153-061-4 (pbk. : alk. paper)
    1. Mission of the church. 2. Presbyterian Church -- Doctrines.
I. Gilliss, Martha S. II. Title
BV601.8.C35 2006
285".137 -- dc22   2005035560

Contents

Foreword

It is a pleasure to invite readers to join Elizabeth Caldwell as she shepherds us through the second great end of the church, the *Shelter, Nurture, and Spiritual Fellowship of the Children of God*. All six of the books in the Great Ends of the Church series[1] share the same aim: to make available for members of our congregations interpretations of what Joseph Small has identified as mission statements for our church. As mission statements, the six great ends present a "holistic vision of the church's life."[2] They have functioned collectively to hold before the Presbyterian Church throughout the twentieth century and now into the twenty-first what our ministry is to be as the body of Christ.

As spelled out in the *Book of Order*, the great ends of the church are: proclamation of the gospel for the salvation of mankind; shelter, nurture, and spiritual fellowship of the children of God; maintenance of divine worship; preservation of the truth; promotion of social righteousness; and exhibition of the Kingdom of Heaven to the world (G-1.0200). Like the other great ends, this one is woven with the others into a single fabric comprising the church's calling. Like the others, it cannot be investigated on its own apart from the other ends. Shelter, nurture, and spiritual fellowship is an end to which all members of a congregation are equally called. Compared with preservation of the truth, proclamation of the gospel, and maintenance of divine worship, ends that are more the purview of those called to ordained ministry; or exhibition of the kingdom of heaven and even promotion of social righteousness, ends that often seem like a steep calling; this mission end is accessible to all. All children of God necessarily find ourselves engaged simply by virtue of gathering together as a congregation. As we share our stories of faith, we are supporting and nurturing one another. Our fellowship grows more solid and firm as we participate in relationships formed around worship and praise of God.

In *Shelter, Nurture, and Spiritual Fellowship of the Children of God*, Caldwell recovers this mission statement from the mists of abstraction and brings it into focus around a true experience of a congregation that she knows well. She takes images from this experience as well as others common to all congregations to help us see what our

Presbyterian forebears had in mind as they drew up this timeless end. She does this by widening the context in which we are to understand it, stretching it back to the days of our father and mother of faith, Abraham and Sarah, who set out on the journey that was their particular response to God's call for their lives.

Caldwell uses the tools of Scripture and two modern confessions to help us to see the eternal roots of this end and how it timelessly will continue to guide our church into the future. In these times of great social change and what some see as dissolution of traditional values, the guidelines for proper procedure are written less in black and white and more in shades of gray. Yet, we are immersed through the power of the Holy Spirit in the potential for taking on this mission joyfully. God continues to form us as we share the gospel's good news and live out its truth among ourselves and as we journey out into our communities and into the broader world.

What once was known as "Christian education" is now often called "Christian formation." This change indicates the Mainline Church's intention to recognize the multidimensional nature of educating Christians—it is an embodied process that makes a claim on the whole person. Christian nurture is not reducible to one hour or less on Sunday mornings. It engages the mind as well as the spirit and the body. Baptism, the Sacrament of the Lord's Supper, making room for prayer at home, mealtimes, understanding Presbyterian polity, working on a Habitat for Humanity house, studying a text in Scripture, hearing a sermon, taking a meal to a shut-in member of the congregation—all are ways in which God educates us about who God is and God's purposes for us in the world.

Being educated about God inevitably means that we have to notice and participate in the ministry to which Christ calls us, as the Holy Spirit opens our hearts and ears and eyes and minds to discern. Sometimes this is against our own wishes. As Caldwell writes, "God's Word to God's people has always been a startling truth, one that creation has not always been ready to hear, to believe, or to accept" (p. 86). This is why this book is such a valuable aid to the learning process, which begins early in our lives but never ends until the day we die, when as the Apostle Paul tells us, "we will then see face to face" (1 Cor. 13:12). Until that time we are nurtured through the joyous and the difficult by our faith communities. To this end is the church's second great end, "the shelter, nurture, and spiritual fellowship of the children of God."

Martha S. Gilliss
Editor, Witherspoon Press
Presbyterian Church (U.S.A.)

Notes

1. Already available from Witherspoon Press: *Proclamation of the Gospel for the Salvation of Humankind* (Catherine Gunsalus González, 2003), *Preservation of the Truth* (Joseph D. Small, 2005), *Maintenance of Divine Worship* (Howard, L. Rice, Jr., 2006).
2. Joseph D. Small, *Preservation of the Truth* (Louisville: Witherspoon Press, 2005), 2.

———

Introduction

The opportunity to write a book on one of the great ends of the church, namely the one that identifies one of the important aspects of mission of the Presbyterian Church as "the shelter, nurture, and spiritual fellowship of the children of God," took on different meaning after September 17, 2003. When asked to write on this particular great end, my mind raced with thinking of the possibilities for engaging with the words "shelter, nurture, and spiritual fellowship" as descriptors of things we are supposed to do with and for the children of God. And I wondered where to begin, with the subject of the great end—the children of God, or with the activities—shelter, nurture, and spiritual fellowship. And it was in that in-between time of creative mulling that September 17 happened.

Few telephone calls at 5:00 a.m. bring good news, and this call was the voice of my sister saying, "The church is on fire; I'm on my way there." The next call was no better, "I'm standing here watching the steeple burn, Lib. We were so close; we had almost made it." Two years prior to this their pastor had resigned for another call. The faithful work of their Pastor Nominating Committee had come to fruition, and the church had called a new pastor who was in the process of moving with his family to their new home. "We almost made it," she said. "And now this."

The shelter, the visible symbol, of their spiritual home was burning in front of her, and the firefighters were standing back unable to approach close enough because of the heat and intensity of the fire. Finally, they were able to approach the building, and water touched the steeple, now stripped of its façade, leaving only the metal structure. The fire was extinguished just below the still-visible cross on top.

At 6:00 p.m. on that same day, the congregation slowly came together as community on the lawn in folding chairs, facing the still-smoldering fire and what remained of the sanctuary, the white brick walls, for a brief service of Witness to the Resurrection. The children of God gathered—teenagers with tears in their eyes, children running up to the church to check on their newly built playground and finding it was okay. An older adult came carrying his own lawn chair. People were standing in small groups, speaking softly, holding each other. Two fathers of elementary age children said, "Let's build the Peaceable Kingdom [the elementary church school] back just the way it was." People who had not been in worship during the interim time somehow found their way back on this day.

Some were able to look ahead. A member of the church who is an artist started visioning a work of art for a new sanctuary that would be created from the ashes of the previous shelter—the twisted copper organ pipes and other debris from the fire. Some could be heard saying, "We can rebuild." I remembered the words of my friend whom I called before getting on the road, affirming, "Lib, I remember burning churches. You can burn a building, but you can't burn a church."

"Do not be afraid, I am the first and the last, and the living one" (Rev. 1:17).

"Do not fear, for I am with you, do not be afraid, for I am your God" (Isa. 41:10a).

"I will strengthen you, I will help you" (Isa. 41:10b).

"I will uphold you with my victorious right hand" (Isa. 41:10c).

Words of Scripture reminded this congregation of its true shelter and its true nurture.

We think of shelter, nurture, and spiritual fellowship in very visible and concrete terms, such as buildings, programs, classes, gatherings, shelter for homeless guests, rooms for community groups, or retreats. But on that Wednesday in September, shelter, nurture, and spiritual fellowship were experienced differently. This was true, too, on the days immediately following. The federal agent from the Bureau of Alcohol, Tobacco, and Firearms (ATF) gave advanced warning that the steeple would need to come down. There were discussions about how they would take off the cross and give it to a church member. On Friday a crane removed the steeple. The cross was taken off, a young firefighter carried it to a small group of church staff and members, and the circle gathered in prayer. On Sunday morning the congregation worshiped under a tent, with flowers provided by the Muslim congregation and food by sister Presbyterian churches, including the new Korean congregation that had used this church for their first church home, a shelter before constructing their own.

This congregation experienced shelter, nurture, and spiritual fellowship in ways they could never have imagined. Two church officers who chaired the property committee immediately assumed new roles as media liaisons and coordinators of the rebuilding process. The head of the cleaning service was allowed access to the undamaged building and started work in the preschool rooms and children's library. She told my sister that the Jesus doll and the other stuffed animals used in worship during the children's time were fine but would need to be cleaned. A neighbor of the church who had helped with building the playground called to volunteer with meals for the federal agents. Children at the nearby Methodist church made pictures with mirrors that read, "God loves you," which they gave to every child in the church. One child drew a picture of a hug for my sister because he knew she would need one.

My sister is the church educator, and she lost her office in this fire, as did the pastors and the office staff. The elementary age children lost their church schoolrooms, their choir room, their musical instruments, and the wooden toys that entertained them in worship. Senior Citizens lost their space for day care and meals-on-wheels, and Room in the Inn lost beds and sheets and space for sheltering homeless. AA and Alanon groups from the community lost their meeting space. And all the children of God lost their sanctuary, their worship home.

Talking with the children of God in worship under the tent on the Sunday after the fire, my sister reminded everyone that the next few years would be an awesome adventure, but that also, because the fire didn't allow time to pack some things, occasionally we would be sad when we looked for something that was no longer there, like a favorite pew, or a favorite room in the Peaceable Kingdom. She confessed, "There may be days when we feel a little lost, but wherever we go on our adventure, God knows our names, and God knows how to bring us home." Her prayer was this: "Thank you, God, that you were with us at the beginning of our adventure, that you will be with us in the middle, and that you will be at the end, to welcome us home. Amen." In that time for children, which really became a time for all God's children, we remembered that Abraham and Sarah went out, not knowing, into their future.

The great ends are mission statements that express the hopes and intentions of the church for its work in the world. Joseph Small has written, "Perhaps mission statements are more like expressions of hope than descriptions of reality. Mission statements may function best in the church when they hold out challenging possibilities, calling a particular Christian community to renewed faith and faithfulness."[1] This book will provide a chapter on each of the concepts included in this particular great end of the church. It will begin at the end with "the who"—all God's children—and then move to those activities that are to be our focus—shelter, nurture, and spiritual fellowship.

Each chapter will begin with a focus on biblical texts and a connection with appropriate parts of two of our most recent confessions of faith, *A Brief Statement of Faith*, written after the reunion of the Presbyterian Church U.S. and the United Presbyterian Church in the USA, and *A Declaration of Faith*, a faith statement of the Presbyterian Church U.S. In addition to focusing on biblical texts and confessional statements, each chapter will follow a similar outline that considers challenging possibilities, expressions of hope, and ways we shape faith and faithfulness as we shelter, nurture, and provide spiritual fellowship for all God's children.

Use this book to help you begin to explore the meaning of this missional statement of our church, "the shelter, nurture, and spiritual fellowship of the children of God." Use it for reflection on your own understanding and experiences of living together in what we call church, our faith community. Consider you own life of faith, your ways of being at home with God who is our shelter, who nurtures us from the moment of our first breath until the last one on our lips, and who surrounds us with the children of God of all ages, colors, and faith traditions. Use this study to help you recall biblical affirmations of God who always sustains, of God who is always more than we can imagine. And finally, let this book help you and your congregation consider the ways God is calling you to provide shelter, nurture, and spiritual fellowship in new and transforming ways.

Note

1. Joseph D. Small, "The Great Ends of the Church" *Church Papers* from the Adult Foundational Curriculum (Louisville: Curriculum Publishing, Presbyterian Church (U.S.A), 1997), 4.

Questions for Reflection and Discussion

1. What comes to mind when you think about the mission of the church being the "shelter, nurture, and spiritual fellowship of the children of God"?

2. What are some of the ways your church is involved in this kind of mission?

3. Joseph Small has written, "Perhaps mission statements are more like expressions of hope than descriptions of reality. Mission statements may function best in the church when they hold out challenging possibilities, calling a particular Christian community to renewed faith and faithfulness."

   Consider your congregation's mission statement. Note places that

   • express hope,

   • describe the reality of the context in which your congregation is located and is committed to serving,

   • offer challenging possibilities, and

   • describe possibilities for the community to respond with renewed faith and faithfulness.

4. Caldwell told a story about a congregation who lost the physical shelter of church. What stories come to mind about your church and the ways you have discovered what it means to be a community of faith in mission together?

All God's Children

1

Doors to the church open on Sunday morning and God's people enter. Teenagers find their friends, children run, adults of all ages greet each other, and a baby in the arms of a parent laughs at a grandmother. It is one of the few contexts in our culture where all ages come together in one place.

The Great Ends of the Church were originally composed in 1910 as a statement of mission of the United Presbyterian Church of North America. As part of its constitution, the Great Ends moved with its members in the merger in 1958 with the Presbyterian Church in the United States of America, forming the United Presbyterian Church of the United States of America (UPC USA). And they continued their journey into the reunited Presbyterian Church (U.S.A.), a merger of the UPC USA and the Presbyterian Church in the United States in 1983. Referring to the Great Ends of the Church, James Smylie has written, "In these words, Presbyterians summarized the way they interpreted the challenge of Jesus to his early disciples, and they stated what the church was still called to do at the end of the twentieth century."[1]

Of the six great ends, this one, "the shelter, nurture, and spiritual fellowship of the children of God" is unique. The others focus on those things we are called to do: proclaim the Gospel, preserve truth, promote social righteousness, exhibit the realm of heaven to the world, and maintain worship. But shelter, nurture, and spiritual fellowship imply being, the way we are to live together as a community of faith. When the great ends are read and discussed, they embody the life and teaching of Jesus and the challenge he offered to those who would follow him as his disciple.

Each chapter of this book will focus on one aspect of this great end of the church. Rather than beginning with the tasks of shelter, nurture, and spiritual fellowship, it seems important to begin with the subject of these aspects of ministry, the children of God. One of the realities of American culture in this postmodern world is the separation of age groups. The wonderful picture of people of all ages coming together on Sunday morning that is painted in the first paragraph of this chapter can also present problems and challenges for being God's children together in the life and mission of the congregation.

We come in the door from our separate contexts—from all levels of retirement living, as families with children, single adults of all ages, teenagers, couples who are married, and couples who have made a covenant commitment to each other. We come with varieties of life experiences, the wisdom of age and life learning and the new and critical questions of teenagers. We come from living with those who are like us—kids in school, adults from our particular work settings.

We come having just found the love of our life, or having lost the love of our life. We come having retired from a job or having lost a job that was loved and provided meaning. And we come having started a new career. We come bringing the newest child who has been born or adopted into the family, and we come grieving the loss of a loved one. We come with all the strength and energy of a four-year-old, and we come with aches and pains and life-threatening illnesses.

All of God's children gather in one space for shelter, for nurture, and for spiritual fellowship, which grows through relationships and through participation in the life and mission of the family of faith.

Biblical Images

Two biblical affirmations are central to understanding and living as children of God: God calls us, and we are chosen by God. If we are to claim our place in the family as children of God, the beginning point is an affirmation of who we are in relation to God, an affirmation of belonging and trust.

When Moses questioned God about his ability to lead God's people, saying, "Who am I that I should go to Pharaoh, and bring the Israelites out of Egypt?" (Exod. 3:11), God's response was, "I will be with you" (Exod. 3:12). And when Moses was so bold as to ask God's name, God replied, "I am who I am" or "I will be what I will be" (Exod. 3:14). Commenting on this passage, Kathleen Norris has written:

> God demands a great deal of Moses, of Abraham and Sarah, of Joseph, Jacob, Rebekah, and Leah. This is a God who keeps us asking, who appears in the scriptures as a rock, a woman in labor, an eagle, a warrior, a creator and destroyer, listener and proclaimer, lover and judge—the Great "I Am."[2]

Reading the Psalms provides rich insight into the nature of the relationship between the Creator and the creation. Psalm 103 is a hymn of thanksgiving for the many acts of God's goodness—acts of forgiveness, healing, justice, and mercy. Notable in this Psalm is the repetition of the phrase, "steadfast love," a love that is from "everlasting to everlasting." This love is always near. God's love is like that of a parent, "As a father has compassion for his children, so the Lord has compassion for those who fear him. For he knows how we were made; he remembers that we are dust" (103:13–14). In response to this affirmation of belonging to God, the Psalmist concludes, "Bless the Lord, O my soul" (103:22b).

Psalm 78 is a kind of storytelling Psalm. It recites the history of God's relationship with God's people and begins with a reminder to the hearer to remember and to tell the children of "the glorious deeds of the Lord, and his might, and the wonders that he has done" (78:4). We are to tell this story of God's deeds to our children so they will know to set their hope in God, not forget the works of God, and keep all God's commandments.

This Psalm is a reminder of the nature of God's love and commitment to God's people. Even when their heart was not steadfast toward God, even when they forgot their covenant with God, God, "being compassionate, forgave their iniquity, and did not . . . stir up all his wrath" (78:38). When God's people rebelled and grieved God's heart, God continued to redeem them, saving them from their enemies.

And when God's people were in exile, living in a foreign land, God sent prophets, like Isaiah to remind God's people to whom they belonged and in whom they could place their trust.

Do not fear, for I have redeemed you;
    I have called you by name, you are mine.
When you pass through the waters, I will be with you;
    and through the rivers, they shall not overwhelm you;
when you walk through fire you shall not be burned,
    and the flame shall not consume you.
For I am the LORD your God,
    the Holy One of Israel, your Savior. . . .
Because you are precious in my sight,
    and honored, and I love you, . . .
Do not fear, for I am with you. (Isa. 43:1–5a)

God has chosen us. We belong to God. The story in the Old Testament of God seeking relationship with humankind continues in the New Testament. This affirmation is vividly described in the prologue of the Gospel of John. Through metaphorical images of light and Word, the gospel writer provides his own unique story of the incarnation of God's son in the world. Jesus, the true light, "came to what was his own, and his own people did not accept him. But to all who received him, who believed in his name, he gave power to become children of God, who were born, not of blood or of the will of the flesh or of the will of man, but of God" (John 1:11–13). Through story and images, metaphors and illustrations, the gospel writer testifies to what it means to be a child of God and what God expects from this belonging.

Norris notes, "this is a God who keeps us asking."[3] As revealed in these Old Testament texts, God is also a God who keeps reminding us of belonging and trust. In continuing to affirm our relationship with God as God's children, God reminds us to ask ourselves questions such as: To whom do you belong? In whom do you put your trust? What difference does this make in your life? What difference does this make in your relationship with those around you? Whose neighbor are you?

In 1983, the reunited Presbyterian Church (U.S.A.) appointed a committee to write a confessional statement titled *A Brief Statement of Faith*. This statement was adopted by the church and is included in our *The Book of Confessions*. The statement contains this affirmation:

> We trust in God,
>> whom Jesus called Abba, Father.
> In sovereign love God created the world good
>> and makes everyone equally in God's image,
>>> Male and female, of every race and people,
>> to live as one community.
> But we rebel against God; we hide from our Creator.
>> Ignoring God's commandments,
>> we violate the image of God in others and ourselves,
>>> accept lies as truth,
>> exploit neighbor and nature,
>> and threaten death to the planet entrusted to our care.
>> We deserve God's condemnation.
> Yet God acts with justice and mercy to redeem creation.

In everlasting love,
>> the God of Abraham and Sarah chose a covenant people
>> to bless all families of the earth.
Hearing their cry,
>> God delivered the children of Israel
>> from the house of bondage.
Loving us still,
>> God makes us heirs with Christ of the covenant.
Like a mother who will not forsake her nursing child,
like a father who runs to welcome the prodigal home,
>> God is faithful still.[4]

Notice this portion begins with an affirmation of trust in God. It goes on to tell the story of God's relationship with humankind. In spite of the many ways that we forget God and God's covenant, God's love is ever faithful, ever sure. Consider the verbs that make clear the nature of God's commitment to belonging to those whom God has created: acts with justice and mercy, chose, hears their cry, delivers, loves, makes us heirs, loves like a mother and a father, and is always faithful.

A Declaration of Faith makes a similar affirmation of God's relationship with humankind.

God moves in history with [God's] people.
Jesus Christ stands at the center of the biblical record.
The Bible is the account of God's word and action in history,
together with God's people's response in faith.
It tells how the Lord has moved with Israel and the church
towards the kingdom of God,
[God's] just and loving rule over all.
It is the story of the one God,
who is the Father, the Son, and the Holy Spirit.
That story is still unfolding
and in faith we make it our own.
It forms our memory and our hope.
It tells us who we are and what we are to do.
To retell it is to declare what we believe.[5]

A Declaration of Faith reminds us, the children of God, that in claiming to belong to God, in claiming to belong to the story of God's people in all their acts of faithfulness and unfaithfulness in the past, we add our story to their story. We place our trust in the assurance of God's love in the present and in the future. In so doing we discover who we are and what we are called to be and do in this world.

As children of God, we belong to God. As children of God we trust in God. These are such simple yet complex affirmations of identity and calling! The last lines of *A Declaration of Faith* make explicit that when we as children of God make this affirmation of identity as being God's own, we are formed differently. The very act of accepting the identity of belonging to God as God's child assumes a relation of trust, and as the statement says, our formation is not cultural but faithful. Claimed as God's own, our response becomes one of memory of whose we are, as well as a life lived in hope for a future that is faithful and lived in response to our identity as God's own child.

God's work is unfinished. God's story of redemption and grace, of steadfast love and mercy, of forgiveness, and new life is always a new story, one that is unfolding as we live in response to God's call, trusting in the promises of God. When we retell this story with the living of our lives, we "declare what we believe."

Challenging Possibilities

There are many challenging possibilities presented to us in our relationship as children of God living together in communities of faith. Recalling the statement in *A Declaration of Faith*, we remember that the story of our relationship with God "is still unfolding and in faith we make it our own. It forms our memory and our hope. It tells us who we are and what we are to do. To retell it is to declare what we believe."[6] These questions come to mind:

- Who are we as children of God gathered within a faith community?
- How do we live with difference in communities of faith, connecting across generations, ideologies, and faith traditions?

Most congregations reflect the realities of the nature of family in today's world. Families do look different from how they looked thirty years ago. Parents may be a mother and a father, a single parent, or two partners of the same sex. Some children grow up being raised by an extended family of relatives. Children in a family may be biological and adopted. Some families are blended because of divorce or other family circumstances.

Take a look around the worship space in your congregation. Observe the seating patterns. Grandparents bring their grandchildren to church because their own children are not involved in the life of the church. Some children grow up participating in two faith traditions, such as Christian and Jewish or Protestant and Catholic, and they come to church with one parent. Children whose parents share joint custody after a divorce may come to church on an irregular basis. Couples who divorce and stay in the same congregation may work out ways to sit together with their children. Single adults sometimes struggle to find their place within a congregation, especially when "family" is defined as couples with children.

With all this difference of lifestyle represented within a congregation, it is no wonder that some may long for another time when roles and relationships were more easily defined and understood. Who makes up a couple is an issue that is dividing both church and nation. Presbyterian congregations who have identified themselves as More Light,[7] and those congregations who welcome all persons regardless of age or sexual identity into the life of their community, are seeking to live out a commitment to ministry with and for all God's children. Other congregations are very clear that a homosexual lifestyle is not biblical, and that persons who live openly and in committed relationships as gay men and lesbians are not welcome in their church.

Who are we as children of God gathered within a faith community? The reality is that we come together as God's children from very many places in life and in many forms or configurations. And together we struggle with two essential theological concepts: calling and chosen. "I have called you by name, you are mine" (Isa. 43:1). *A Brief Statement of Faith* reminds us that "God created the world good and makes everyone equally in God's image, male and female, of every race and people, to live as one community."[8]

In 2000, the movie *Chocolat* told the story of a woman who arrived with her daughter in a small French town and set up a chocolate shop. The hospitality of her shop made it a community for many who were outsiders in the small town: the aged, the abused, the lonely. It became a welcoming congregation for God's children in ways that the local Catholic Church did not. The young priest Pere Henri was supervised by one of the church leaders. His sermons were carefully edited to say what the church leader wanted him to preach. Finally at Easter, the young priest found his voice in his homily.

I do not know what the theme of my homily today ought to be. Do I want to talk about the miracle of our Lord's divine transformation? Not really, no. I don't want to talk about His divinity. I'd rather talk about His humanity. I mean, you know, how He lived His life here on earth. His kindness, His tolerance . . . Listen, here's what I think. I think we can't go 'round measuring our goodness by what we don't do, what we deny ourselves, what we resist, and who we exclude. I think we've got to measure goodness by what we embrace, what we create, and who we include.[9]

A Declaration of Faith tells us that the biblical story evolves, unfolds as we hear it, as we retell it to a new generation, as "we make it our own." As we live our lives in response to God's call, we are formed by the story of God's faithful actions in the lives of God's people. As Pere Henri reminded his congregation, we declare what we believe by what we embrace, what we create, and whom we include.

In reflecting on the concept of being chosen by God, Kathleen Norris has said written:

When others label me and try to exclude me, as too conservative or too liberal, as too feminist or not feminist enough, as too intellectual or not intellectually rigorous, as too Catholic to be a Presbyterian or too Presbyterian to be a Catholic, I refuse to be shaken from the fold. It's my God, too, my Bible, my church, my faith; it chose me. But it does not make me "chosen" in a way that would exclude others. I hope it makes me eager to recognize the good, and the holy, wherever I encounter it.[10]

Who are we as children of God gathered within a faith community? As A Brief Statement of Faith implies, from the youngest child welcomed into the life of the faith community to the oldest church member, we are "heirs with Christ of the covenant."[11] God, the loving parent, God who is mother and father of us all, calls us into community and chooses to be in relationship with God's creation in abiding steadfast love and faithfulness.

A second challenging possibility for the children of God is to consider our response to this question: How do we live with difference in communities of faith, connecting across generations, ideologies, and faith traditions? Church members who are lifelong Presbyterians are in a minority today. No longer can we assume a common theological perspective and ecclesiological background. Our congregations are filled with people who may have experiences of a variety of previous faith traditions or have no church background.

In describing the challenge of being Christian in a pluralist culture, American church historian Martin Marty has called many of those who participate in Christian education "refugees, exiles, or rebels."[12] Our congregations are filled with people who come to our doors seeking a welcome place, a place of comfort and support for their questions of faith, their struggles with making sense of the world. Are we able to welcome children of God who have been exiled from another faith tradition? Are we able to welcome children of God who come with different perspectives, different theological beliefs? Time will tell whether it is possible for us to continue as Presbyterians to practice our faith with this diversity of biblical and theological perspectives. Some may think that would surely be easier to split along theological lines across denominations so that we could be with those who think like we do. I am sure that is a prayer that many pray.

During the fall of 2004, I taught a course on Faith and the Ballot Box with a member of the ministry staff at my church. We began with an explanation that the class would be about issues of the election, such as health care, education, immigration, terrorism, and the response of Christians. It would not be a class debate between Republicans and Democrats. We all tried to hide our political alliances, which was not always easy or possible. The class met for eight weeks, and the last class was the Sunday after the election. Some came to that last class admitting they had not wanted to be there because they were so upset about the election results. Some were experiencing feelings of anger, grief, and loss. Others came confident that the will of the people had been heard and that the country would be in good hands with the continuing leadership.

By reflecting on that experience, I realized how important it is for the children of God to come together from diverse places in the world to listen and to speak, to make room for silence and to hear a word from the Lord. It was not easy sometimes to share that space together, but it was very important to be there. Each week we closed with a reading of the Psalm for the day and prayer, inviting each person to let the words of the Psalmist move deeply within them as they continued to reflect on God's call to their life.

Perhaps the greatest challenge to the church today is diversity— of faith tradition, of beliefs, of understandings of family, of how we interpret Scripture, of how we worship, and of what music we use. Related to that is the challenge of planning for worship and educational ministry and mission with people across the life span from the youngest to the oldest.

Truly our churches are places where we come to hear the "Word of the Lord," where we come to be challenged out of the complacency of our lives, to hear again in new ways God's Word for us. Is there room for all, both those who are at home with their faith and those who are in exile, to hear again God's Word?

The story is told of a young seminarian serving a small Presbyterian congregation in upstate New York. Shortly after he arrived, church members handed him the Scripture lessons for the coming Sunday and told him to preach on them. At first he was offended that they didn't want to know what he had to say. The church members told him that "what we want to know is, is there a word from the Lord? You see, life is tough here. Our neighbors and friends are losing their farms. Inflation is killing us. There's no work for our young. They had to leave. . . . Listen and see if there is a word from the Lord."[13]

The young student thought they were a bit crazy. He was thinking, "A word from the Lord? Are you crazy? What is this?"

> "This," the members of his new congregation might have answered, "is church. This is what church is, people created by the Word, people sustained by the Word, people who wait for a word from God. We're not all that interested in you and what you have to say. Our need is too deep for that. We need God."[14]

The world in which we live appears smaller as our technology continues to grow. Images of war and terrorism, abuse, and the horrors of our sin and inhumanity to God's creation fill our ears, our eyes, indeed, all of our senses. We bring the wounds of the world with us as we walk into church on Sunday morning. Like the people in the small congregation in upstate New York, we come as God's children seeking a word from the Lord. This is the commonality that binds together God's children living together in a community of faith.

Expressions of Hope

Mission statements are a way for congregations and denominations to articulate both their identity and their purpose, to communicate an inspiring vision of faith and action. As such, by their very nature they are expressions of hope, the ways in which a community of faith or a denomination seeks to live faithfully in the world. Two expressions of hope for the children of God are the sacraments of baptism and Eucharist.

In writing about the sacrament of baptism, theologian John Burkhart has said that "no community is ever the same after it has been invaded by the new."[15] In an article on pastoral care and baptism, Herbert Anderson reminds us that the nature and function of this sacrament is one of initiation with two actions: incorporating and individuating. It is both an event and a process. Anderson says that baptism both expresses and celebrates "God's work among us in making all things new."[16] He believes there are three important tasks: creating a welcoming environment, creating a holding environment, and supporting a believing environment.[17]

A baptism is a welcome with water. It enfolds the newest into a community of faith and invites this person to grow. A welcome with the water of baptism implies there is "both space and time for nurture."[18] What are the ways this welcoming aspect of baptism is embodied in your congregation?

- Are children and youth welcome in worship as participants and as leaders—as liturgists, ushers, musicians, and artists?
- Are children welcome to participate in mission projects of the church?
- Are children welcome at the Lord's Table?
- Are the time and talents of children and youth honored in the same ways as those of adults? How are they invited to use them?
- Whose children are welcome in our congregations?
- In what ways are congregational life and worship designed to nurture the spiritual lives of children and youth?

The second task of baptism is one of creating a holding environment for growth in the life of the Christian faith. It is a balance between holding on and letting go, that most basic of developmental tasks. To walk, a baby has to let go of the coffee table or your hand and take those first, shaky steps. And once that first step has been taken, a child's environment is forever changed. She can walk where she wants to go. But a parent is always behind her watching where she goes so no harm comes her way.

Just as with the first steps of walking, a holding environment for faith must have a balance between freedom and safety. In *The Courage To Teach*, Parker Palmer writes about the importance of the environment of teaching and learning as being both hospitable and charged; it must be inviting, open, safe, a place of trust, yet also a place of challenge, and risk taking. Palmer says that a classroom "must not feel so safe that [students] fall asleep."[19] And so, too, the congregation.

If the congregation is a place where faith in God is both awakened and nurtured, it is at the same time a place where we learn how to live as God's children. Within the gentle holding arms of church members, we are invited to grow and we are invited to ask our questions, to share our doubts, and to take risks. We are invited to engage the biblical text and struggle with God "who executes justice for the orphan and the widow, and who loves the strangers, providing them food and clothing" (Deut. 10:18). And we are invited into the risky place of living in response to God's commandment that "You shall also love the stranger, for you were strangers in the land of Egypt" (Deut. 10:19).

- Which families do we nurture and support in this holding environment of the community of faith? Mother and father and child? Single mothers or fathers? Parents of children who are adopted? Committed same-sex partners and their biological or adopted child? Grandparents who are raising their grandchildren? Divorced parents who both decide to stay in the congregation? Parents of children with handicapping conditions—mental, physical, or emotional?
- In what ways are our congregations "holding environments that prepare us for service" in God's world, teaching us how to be disciples?[20]
- In what ways are our congregations providing room to grow as an environment that is both hospitable and charged— supporting and challenging for the living of our faith in this world?

The third task in relation to baptism is to become a believing environment. In contrast to baptism as a social rite or familial tradition, Presbyterians believe that baptism is an act of faith on the part of parents or a parent and a congregation. The family is "a believing environment" in several ways, according to Anderson. First, because it has made the decision to have or adopt a child; second, in the way that it teaches the child to hope and to trust; and finally, because "its life always points beyond itself to Christ and the world for which Christ died."[21]

Being Presbyterian and Reformed means that we believe in the communal celebration of the sacraments within the context of worship. As a family is forever changed by the birth or adoption of a child, so too the congregation is changed as a child is incorporated into its body.

Baptism is both incorporating and individuating. It welcomes an individual with water into a community of faith. It is an act of faith by a believing community that makes promises for the lifetime of the child. Baptism is both an event and a process. A welcome with water invites the newest one to live in faith for a lifetime, until the last breath is taken and baptism is complete.

- What marks your congregation as a believing environment?
- In what ways is your congregation involved in helping parents claim their vocation as faith educators of their child/children?
- In what ways are members of the congregation held accountable to the promises they make at a baptism?

I love singing baptismal hymns. There are only seven in *The Presbyterian Hymnal*. (In contrast there are twenty-four hymns for the sacrament of the Lord's Supper.) I have noticed that some churches select one baptismal hymn, which they use every time. Others have a special refrain that is sung, and in some churches the choir sings a response. And yet others never sing a baptismal hymn. "Wash, O God, Our Sons and Daughters" is one of my favorites. It helps me connect the baptismal act of blessing with water and the spoken words. Holding the child, the baptismal waters still fresh on her head, the minister often concludes with these words: "You are sealed by the Holy Spirit in your baptism and you belong to Jesus Christ forever."

Ruth Duck, who wrote this hymn, has been a friend of mine since high school days in Memphis, Tennessee. I was talking with her about this hymn, sharing that I was intrigued with the line, "weave them garments bright and sparkling; compass them with love and light." Compass them, she said, was her attempt to think of a poetical way to say encompass them, surround them. I like "compass them." O God, be like a compass for this child, showing them paths to follow.

The Eucharist, or the sacrament of the Lord's Supper, is equally an expression of hope for the children of God. Having been welcomed with water into a community of faith, the children of God are fed a meal at the Table where Jesus Christ is the host. The liturgy for the Lord's Table begins with an invitation, a welcome to all children, youth, adults, and all who trust in Jesus as their Lord and Savior, to share in this meal of bread and cup. It is a meal of both memorial acclamation as well as feast, or joyful celebration of hope and promise.

I was teaching an adult class and we were discussing homosexuality and the church and the position of the Presbyterian Church on the ordination of gay men and lesbians, an issue that is dividing many denominations today. One person said that she believed it to be very important that our polity be changed to allow any one called by God to serve as officer or minister, regardless of their sexual orientation. She went on to say that she believed this so strongly that she would find it impossible to eat a meal with someone who did not agree. I suggested to her that every time she comes to the Lord's Table in this church she probably shares a meal with someone who disagrees with her.

Our polity does make clear who is welcome at Christ's Table:

> All the baptized faithful are to be welcomed to the Table, and none shall be excluded because of race, sex, age, economic status, social class, handicapping condition, difference of culture or language, or any barrier created by human injustice. . . . Each time they gather at the Table the believing community: (a) are united with the Church in every place, and the whole Church is present; (b) join with all the faithful in heaven and on earth in offering thanksgiving to the triune God; (c) renew the vows taken at Baptism; and they commit themselves afresh to love and serve God, one another, and their neighbors in the world.[22]

Notice the four acts of the sacrament. In coming to the Table, we are united with Christians in every time and place and through the ages, so that we have a taste of the Church that is larger than that which we experience Sunday after Sunday in our own particular contexts.

In coming to the Table we join faithful Christians in giving thanks to God who is our Creator, Redeemer, and Sustainer. We come to the Table, putting aside our differences and for a moment stand together affirming the faith in which we live and move and have our being.

We come to the Table having been marked by the waters of our baptism, named and claimed in faith and in the act of breaking bread and sharing cup, we say again what we believe, "This is the bread of life, given for you. . . . This is the cup of the new covenant given for you for the forgiveness of sins."

And finally we come together at the Table in prayers of thanksgiving for what God has done in Jesus Christ, and we renew our commitments to being faithful disciples in God's world.

It is a Table that is larger than our personal preferences for community. It is a Table that calls us to live into the challenging possibilities of being Jesus' disciples in this world. It is a Table that is an expression of hope of a community that lives in response to their baptism. It is a Table without borders or fences where anyone who professes their faith in Jesus Christ as Lord and Savior is welcome. It is a Table where all are welcome, not for the complexity of their beliefs or the amount of knowledge they possess but because they can say, "I am a child of God. I belong to Jesus Christ forever." It is a Table of diversity where we grow in our understanding as we mature in the life of the Christian faith.

Sacraments are expressions of hope for the children of God. Recall the words used in the liturgy of the Lord's Table: "Every time you eat this bread and drink this cup, you proclaim the saving death of the risen Lord, until he comes."[23]

Remember the questions asked at a baptism:

1. Trusting in the gracious mercy of God, do you turn from the ways of sin and renounce evil and its power in the world?
2. Do you turn to Jesus Christ and accept him as your Lord and Savior, trusting in his grace and love?
3. Will you be Christ's faithful disciple, obeying his Word and showing his love?[24]

And then while the baptismal waters are still freshly visible on the head of the one being baptized, the minister says, "You are sealed by the Holy Spirit in your baptism and you belong to Jesus Christ forever."

Together these sacraments become embedded within human beings as a grammar of faith, a way to put together the experience of faith and life. Truly they are expressions of hope for the children of God gathered in community as church.

Shaping Faith and Faithfulness

In May of 2004, Fourth Presbyterian Church in Chicago celebrated the ninetieth anniversary of the dedication of its sanctuary. The first structure was dedicated in 1871 and had one worship service before the great fire of Chicago destroyed it that evening. The congregation relocated on vacant land near Lake Michigan before there was a bridge over the river on Michigan Avenue. An architect was hired, and the

Architectural Record described the new sanctuary as "a living, breathing, spiritual thing . . . a marvel of grace, beauty, and dignity."[25]

At one of the services of dedication in 1904, James G. K. McClure, the President of McCormick Theological Seminary said this:

> My soul's desire and prayer to God for this church is that its heart may be like unto the heart of God, that heart that loves every child of earth. . . . O, that this church may be bigger than any one creed, sect or class or race or color. May it be so big that any human being may feel at home here, may draw nigh to God here. May it be the mission of this church to tell every person in unmistakable terms how dear they are—preciously dear—to God, and then to live those words in the magnanimity of its welcome, the warmth of its fellowship, and the generosity of its devotion.[26]

How timely these words and hopes are for us in this new millennium! May all our churches be living, breathing, spiritual things. . . . marvels of grace, beauty, and dignity. May our congregations be so big that all children, all youth, and all adults may feel welcomed within our doors and may draw close to God there. May our welcome extend beyond the doors of our churches into our communities and the world so that all people may know how dear they are to God, how loved they are.

Notes
1. James H. Smylie, *A Brief History of the Presbyterians* (Louisville: Geneva Press, 1996), 151.
2. Kathleen Norris, *Amazing Grace: Vocabulary of Faith* (New York: Riverhead Books, 1998), 111.
3. Ibid.
4. *A Brief Statement of Faith*, lines 27–51, in The Constitution of the Presbyterian Church (U.S.A.), Part I, *The Book of Confessions* (Louisville: Office of the General Assembly, 2002).
5. *A Declaration of Faith*, chapter 1 section 4, at www.pcusa.org/theologyandworship/worship/decoffaith.pdf.
6. Ibid.
7. More Light is a designation for those churches that identify themselves with this organization within the PC(USA), an organization that works for the inclusion of all people, regardless of sexual orientation.
8. *A Brief Statement of Faith*, lines 29–32.
9. *Chocolat*, directed by Lasse Hallström (Miramax, 2001).
10. Norris, *Amazing Grace*, 143.
11. *A Brief Statement of Faith*, line 48.

12. Martin E. Marty, "Christian Education in a Pluralistic Culture," in *Rethinking Christian Education: Explorations in Theory and Practice*, ed. David S. Schuller (St. Louis: Chalice Press, 1993), 22.

13. Martin B. Copenhaver, Anthony B. Robinson, and William H. Willimon, *Good News in Exile: Three Pastors Offer a Hopeful Vision for the Church* (Grand Rapids: Eerdmans, 1999), 40.

14. Ibid., 41.

15. John E. Burkhart, *Worship* (Louisville: Westminster John Knox Press, 1982), 134.

16. Herbert Anderson, "Pastoral Care in the Process of Initiation" in *Alternative Futures for Worship, vol. 2, Baptism and Confirmation*, ed. Mark Searle (Collegeville, MN: Liturgical Press, 1987), 106.

17. Ibid.

18. Ibid.

19. Parker J. Palmer, *The Courage to Teach: Exploring the Inner Landscape of a Teacher's Life* (San Francisco: Jossey-Bass, 1998), 75.

20. Anderson, 119.

21. Anderson, 106.

22. *Book of Order: The Constitution of the Presbyterian Church (U.S.A.), Part II* (Louisville: Office of the General Assembly, 2004/2005), W-2.4006.

23. *Book of Common Worship*, Office of Theology and Worship, Presbyterian Church (U.S.A.) (Louisville: Westminster John Knox Press, 1993), 69.

24. Ibid., 407.

25. John Buchanan, "Christ Incognito," Fourth Presbyterian Church, Chicago (May 16, 2004). The quote is from the *Architectural Record* vol. XXXVI, no. 3 (Sept. 1914), 179.

26. From the Historical Service to dedicate the new building of the Fourth Presbyterian Church of Chicago, May 12, 1914.

27. Smylie, 151.

Questions for Reflection and Discussion

1. In describing the Great Ends of the Church, Presbyterian historian James Smylie has said: "In these words, Presbyterians summarized the way they interpreted the challenge of Jesus to his early disciples, and they stated what the church was still called to do at the end of the twentieth century."[27] Where in the Gospels do you find Jesus challenging his disciples with regards to this great end of shelter, nurture, and spiritual fellowship of all God's children?

2. *A Declaration of Faith* affirms that the story of the relationship of God with the creation is "still unfolding and in faith we make it our own." In what ways is this story unfolding in the life of your congregation?

3. Read together the parts of *A Brief Statement of Faith* and *A Declaration of Faith* that are included here. Look for ways that

God and God's relationship with humankind are described. What do these contemporary faith statements affirm about being a child of God?

4. Caldwell cites a number of biblical references that describe the relationship of God to humankind. What other biblical texts are important to your understanding of this relationship?

5. How would you describe who you are as the children of God gathered within this faith community?

6. In what ways does your congregation live with difference, connecting across generations, ideologies, and faith traditions?

7. In what ways is your congregation challenged by living with difference?

8. In the section Expressions of Hope, consider the questions that are asked about who is welcome:

   • In what ways are children and youth welcomed in worship—as participants, as leaders—liturgists, ushers, musicians, and artists?

   • In what ways are children welcome to participate in mission projects of the church?

   • Are children welcome at the Lord's Table?

   • Are the time and talents of children and youth honored in the same ways as those of adults? How are they invited to use them?

   • Whose children are welcome in our congregations?

9. In what ways are congregational life and worship designed to nurture the spiritual lives of children, youth, and adults?

10. Of the three tasks—creating a welcoming environment, creating a holding environment, and supporting a believing environment—which is most in evidence in your congregation? Which could be improved?

11. Discuss your congregation's practice of the Lord's Supper in light of the description of this sacrament. In what ways are they similar or different?

12. If you could complete this sentence, what would you say? "My soul's desire and prayer to God for this church is . . ." Invite those who are willing to share their response to do so.

Shelter

2

I worship in an urban Presbyterian congregation. When it opens its doors, in addition to its members, strangers wander in off the streets, some in need of a meal, some visiting the city for the weekend, and some in need of a back row to sit in and warm up from the cold winter wind. The doors open and persons from all kinds of faith traditions look for a seat. The doors open wide to welcome persons who come as they are: single, married, divorced, widowed, or in nontraditional relationships. All are greeted, all are welcomed as God's children. The sanctuary space is open and welcome to the neighboring Jewish congregation for their observance of the high holy days of Rosh Hashanah and Yom Kippur.

What does it mean to talk about the shelter of God's children? What did it mean for those who wrote this statement of mission in the early years of the twentieth century? What does it mean for us at the beginning of the twenty-first century?

The other five great ends of the church speak of the church's mission in terms of things it is to do: proclaim the gospel, maintain worship, preserve truth, promote social righteousness, and exhibit the realm of heaven to the world. These statements provide theological definition for the church's mission both within the congregation and in the world.

So in this particular great end of the church, shelter could reference a physical place, a church building where God's children gather for nurture and spiritual fellowship. Shelter could be that kind of church described at the beginning of this chapter. Yet, it could also have a less physical connotation if we understand shelter as a canopy of faith that surrounds and supports the children of God who come together as a community of faith.

Shelters provide temporary places of rest, such as the structures set up along hiking trails. Many of our congregations participate in community programs of homeless shelters, or "Room in the Inn," places where people who live on the streets can find food and a bed for the night. In times of dangerous weather, such as hurricanes or tornadoes, we seek temporary shelter in safe places with others who have left their homes.

All of these images relate to the notion of temporary space, something we inhabit or dwell in for a short period of time. What about the concept of shelter from a more permanent or lasting perspective? Can we speak of the church—or even of faith—as a shelter for persons who are formed in its community?

And what about the image of God as shelter? The sheltering image of God as parent from *A Brief Statement of Faith* reminds us that "Like a mother who will not forsake her nursing child, like a father who runs to welcome the prodigal home, God is faithful still."[1]

Biblical Images

To speak of the mission of the church as sheltering the children of God brings to mind the biblical themes of hospitality and community and the immanence of God. What does it mean to find shelter in God? What does it mean to provide shelter for others? What biblical models of hospitality inform the ways we shelter God's children today?

The Psalter is probably one of my favorite books in the Bible because the Psalms present a seemingly timeless range of expressions. From songs of praise to communal celebrations, from songs of doubt and questioning to mournful laments, the psalmists capture the depths of humankind's seeking shelter in God. If all we had were the Psalter, we would have a vivid description of God's shelter of God's children.

Psalm 139 speaks of "The Inescapable God" in this way:

> O Lord, you have searched me and known me,
> You know when I sit down and when I rise up;
>> you discern my thoughts from far away.
> You search out my path and my lying down,
>> and are acquainted with all my ways.
> Even before a word is on my tongue,
>> O Lord, you know it completely.
>
>   . . .

Where can I go from your spirit?
> Or where can I flee from your presence?

. . .

If I take the wings of the morning
> and settle at the farthest limits of the sea,
even there your hand shall lead me,
> and your right hand shall hold me fast.

(Ps. 139:1–4, 7, 9–10)

In the psalmist's affirmation of faith and trust, this Psalm vividly captures God's nearness to those whom God has created. Notice how this sheltering relationship is described in terms of how God knows the psalmist. There is no place where this person can go that God is not there as an abiding presence, a shelter.

The prophets called to bear God's message to God's people had direct experience of the immanence of God. In times of great hardship or exile, God's sheltering arms sustained the prophet and gave him words of comfort for the people. Recall the words of God to the prophet Isaiah:

Do not fear, for I have redeemed you;
> I have called you by name, you are mine.
When you pass through the waters, I will be with you;
> and through the rivers, they shall not overwhelm you;
when you walk through fire you shall not be burned;
> and the flame shall not consume you.
For I am the LORD your God, the Holy One of Israel,
> Your Savior.

. . .

Do not fear, for I am with you. (Isa. 43:1b–3a, 5a)

Exiled from their homes and their temple, the Israelites must have wondered where God was. Where was this One who had promised them that "I will be your God and you will be my people"? Where was this One who had promised to love them with a steadfast love? This second part of the book of Isaiah reminds God's children that God is not absent, that even though the shelter of their homes, their city, their community, and their temple is gone, God is present, with them in water and in fire, "Because you are precious in my sight, and honored, and I love you" (Isa. 43:4a).

Elijah, an earlier prophet of the Lord, ran into trouble with his prophecy and fled to the mountains fearing that his life was in danger from Ahab and Jezebel. Elijah escaped into the wilderness and fell asleep. An angel awoke him and told him to get up and eat. Elijah found a cake and a jar of water in front of him. Elijah finally followed the angel's instructions and found safety in a cave on Mt. Horeb. It was there that he heard God's voice, which told him to go out and stand on the mountain because the Lord was going to pass by. In wind and earthquake, and in fire, God's presence was not heard or seen. After the fire there was the "sound of sheer silence" (NRSV) or "a still small voice" (RSV), and Elijah heard God's voice of promise of presence and deliverance (1 Kings 19:12).

Elijah reminded God that he had only been doing what God had asked of him, and now his life was in danger. God's simple instructions were: "Go out and stand on the mountain before the Lord, for the Lord is about to pass by" (1 Kings 19:11a). Elijah did not find God in the loud and tumultuous acts of nature but only in the aftermath of their passing. Elijah's shelter with God was realized in the sound of silence. Silence was where God was found.

In Scripture, to those to whom God revealed God's self, much was expected. The writer of Deuteronomy sums up the essence of the law with these verses:

> So now, O Israel, what does the LORD your God require of you? Only to fear the LORD your God, to walk in all his ways, to love him, to serve the LORD your God with all your heart and with all your soul, and to keep the commandments of the LORD your God and his decrees that I am commanding you today, for your own well-being. . . . For the LORD your God is God of gods and Lord of lords, the great God, mighty and awesome, who is not partial and takes no bribe, who executes justice for the orphan and the widow, and who loves the strangers, providing them food and clothing. You shall also love the stranger, for you were strangers in the land of Egypt. (Deut. 10:12–14, 17–19)

God established a covenant relationship with God's people. Having been chosen and loved and sheltered, God's people were expected to live in response to this steadfast love, caring for others, loving the stranger.

In God's infinite wisdom, this essence of the law came to be incarnated in human form. Morton Kelsey has noted that "our ever-surprising Creator" intimately knew the depths of God's creatures and all that they were capable of doing. God knew as well that human beings respond more by pictures and images and stories than they do by abstract arguments and explanations. All this is expressed by John 3:16. God loved the world so much that God entered into human history and became part of the fabric of our life in such a way that revealed the mercy, love, and forgiveness at the heart of the Divine Creator in a way comprehensible to us.[2]

What biblical models of hospitality inform the ways we shelter God's children today? *A Brief Statement of Faith* expresses its Christ-ological affirmation in this way:

> We trust in Jesus Christ,
>> fully human, fully God.
> Jesus proclaimed the reign of God:
>> preaching good news to the poor
>>> and release to the captives,
>> teaching by word and deed
>>> and blessing the children,
>> healing the sick
>>> and binding up the brokenhearted,
>> eating with outcasts,
>>> forgiving sinners,
>> and calling all to repent and believe the gospel.[3]

At the beginning of his ministry, Jesus went to the synagogue in Nazareth and read from the scroll of Isaiah:

> The Spirit of the Lord is upon me,
>> because he has anointed me to bring good news to the poor.
>> He has sent me to proclaim release to the captives
>> and recovery of sight to the blind,
>> to let the oppressed go free,
> to proclaim the year of the Lord's favor. (Luke 4:18–19)

The words of the prophet became embodied in the actions of God's son, Jesus. *A Brief Statement of Faith* reminds us of Jesus' actions of proclaiming, preaching, teaching, healing, eating, and calling. These same actions are visibly present within the church, a living and breathing shelter for God's people.

A Declaration of Faith affirms the role of community in living our lives in faith in response to the incarnating promises of God.

> God made us for life in community.
> God created human beings with a need for community
> and with freedom to enter into it
> by responding to their Maker with grateful obedience
> and to one another with love and helpfulness.
> We believe that we have been created
> to relate to God and each other
> in freedom and responsibility.
> We may misuse our freedom and deny our responsibility
> by trying to live without God and other people
> or against God and other people.
> Yet we are still bound to them for our life and well-being,
> and intended for free and responsible fellowship with them.
> Since every human being is made
> for communion with God and others,
> we must treat no one with contempt.
> We are to respect and love all other people
> and ourselves as well.[4]

Jesus' disciples came to him with a question, "Who is the greatest in the kingdom of heaven?" Jesus invited a child to come forward from the crowd and said,

> "Truly I tell you, unless you change and become like children, you will never enter the kingdom of heaven. Whoever becomes humble like this child is the greatest in the kingdom of heaven. Whoever welcomes one such child in my name welcomes me." (Matt. 18:3–5)

In his teaching to the crowds that surrounded him toward the end of his ministry, Jesus spoke about the end times when the nations would be held accountable and judged according to their actions. Jesus paints a vivid picture of how God's children will be judged. The people respond with this query: 'Lord, when was it that we saw you hungry or thirsty or a stranger or naked or sick or in prison, and did not take care of you?' Then he will answer them, 'Truly I tell you, just as you did not do it to one of the least of these, you did not do it to me'" (Matt. 25:44–45).

As the faith statement reminds us, "every human being is made for communion with God and others." Welcoming all of God's children, Paul's letter to the church at Galatia tells us: "As many of you as were baptized into Christ have clothed yourselves with Christ. There is no longer Jew or Greek, there is no longer slave or free, there is no longer male and female; for all of you are one in Christ Jesus. And if you belong to Christ, then you are Abraham's offspring, heirs according to the promise (Gal. 3:27–29).

God reveals God's self as the Holy One of Israel who loves humankind with a steadfast love that never fails. This sheltering love of God extends to the communities in which we live. As the faith statement reminds us, we respond to our "Maker with grateful obedience and to one another with love and helpfulness." How big is your shelter?

Challenging Possibilities

How might shelter be understood as a canopy of faith that surrounds and supports the children of God who come together in community? A related question is how this canopy of faith challenges the children of God to consider the ways they welcome a stranger. A shelter needs both windows and doors, windows to let in light and air and doors for hospitality.

An image that has been helpful for me as I think about this notion of shelter involves homemaking. Sharon Daloz Parks writes that,

> Home-making . . . is a connective, creative act of the human imagination and a primary activity of Spirit. It is the creation of forms and patterns which cultivate and shelter life itself. Homemaking and homesteading are activities which build a space where souls can thrive and dream—secure, protected, related, nourished, and whole.[5]

Notice the adjectives Parks uses to describe what souls need in order to thrive and to dream. They need to be secure and protected, related, nourished, and whole.

Just as with the first steps of walking, a holding environment for faith must maintain a balance between freedom and safety. If the congregation is a place where faith in God is both awakened and nurtured, it is at the same time a place where we learn how to be God's people. Within the gentle holding arms of church members, we are invited to grow, to ask our questions, to share our doubts, and to take risks. We are invited to engage the biblical text and struggle with God "who executes justice for the orphan and the widow, and who loves the strangers, providing them food and clothing" (Deut. 10:18). And we are invited into the risky place of living in response to God's commandment that "You shall also love the stranger, for you were strangers in the land of Egypt" (Deut. 10:19).

Mary Pipher is a practicing family therapist who has written about family ecology in *The Shelter of Each Other: Rebuilding Our Families*. In discussing the role of family providing shelter in the face of the competing demands of the culture, Pipher has identified six things that she believes shelter families. These activities provide definition and strength for the family. They include:

1. **Time.** Pipher suggests that simple things, such as limiting activities of individual family members, having a regular mealtime together, having one evening when nothing is scheduled, turning off the television, and not answering the phone during mealtime, are ways that a family can protect time they have together.

2. **Places.** Pipher believes that special or sacred places for a family can be anywhere. She has a preference for outside spaces, such as parks and trails.

3. **Interests.** Sharing something in common, such as love and care for pets, sports, the arts, gardening, or hobbies, are activities that a family can do together that help to shelter and protect the family.

4. **Celebrations.** According to Pipher, "families need celebrations that signify rites of passage. Without these celebrations, time runs together and the significance of events is not noted."[6] Some families create their own celebrations, taking buckets to fill with ripe blueberries in the summer or visiting the pumpkin patch to select just the right one for carving.

5. **Connecting Rituals**. "These rituals connect family to each other, to extended family, to family friends and to the community. They can also connect the old to the young, the rich to the poor, ethnic minorities to ethnic majorities and even the dead to the living."[7]

6. **Stories and Metaphors.** We all have stories that have become part of the family tradition, stories that have to be retold. Pipher believes that "stories reveal what a family wants to believe about itself."[8] She also says that families have metaphors that represent those things that are valued and are important to the family. It can be a place, an activity, or even a food.

When I first saw this list, it was immediately obvious that two things were missing. There are two more things that shelter families, activities that work to make families strong and connected. I would add to her list:

- **Practices of Faith.** Having regular practices of faith such as prayer, reading the Bible, observing the Christian calendar at home, and honoring Sabbath are things that strengthen families and their Christian identity.

- **Participating in a Faith Community.** Active participation in the life of a congregation strengthens, supports, and challenges the life of faith of each family member.

Another way to conceive of shelter is to think about the ways we make a home for faith.[9] Those who are committed to making a home for faith are intentionally focused on being aware of God's activity in their life, God's nearness.

Consider people you know who have no canopy of faith. Having been born and raised in a faithful family, I cannot imagine what it would be like not to be immersed in faith. But I know it is not that way for everyone. The *New York Times* Sunday magazine in January 2004, had an article titled "Coveting Luke's Faith." The author, Dana Tierney, wrote that the literal-minded response to her childhood faith questions like "Angels can fly up in heaven, but how do clouds hold up pianos?" leaves her unable to believe in God. She says, "My friends and relatives who rely on God, the real believers, not just the churchgoers—have an expansiveness of spirit. When they walk along a stream, they don't just see water falling over rocks; the sight fills them with ecstasy. They see a realm of hope beyond this world. I just see a babbling brook. I don't get the message."[10] Although her husband was raised a devout Catholic, Tierney notes that "he doesn't even have the *desire* to believe. So other than baptizing our son to reassure our families, we've skated over the issue of faith. I assumed we had stranded our four-year-old son, Luke, in the same spiritually arid place we'd found ourselves in."[11]

Her husband went to Iraq and she and Luke were watching a program on television one night that told the story of a soldier on leave and how he was afraid to return. Luke's mother looked over to see him steepling his fingers with his head bowed. She asked him what he was doing. Luke did not want to answer. Finally he said, "I was saying a little prayer for Daddy." She told him that was wonderful. She writes, "It was as if that mustard seed of faith had found its way into our son and now he was revealing that he could move mountains. Not in a church or as we gazed at the stars, but while we channel-surfed. I was envious of him. Luke wasn't rattled, because he believed that God would bring his father home safely. I was the only one stranded."[12]

How interesting that the baptismal waters that blessed Luke have not so compassed his mother and his father. But perhaps they may be able to let Luke and his faith be a blessing for them. He has a growing grammar of faith. His mother writes that "After I saw Luke praying for his father in Iraq, I asked him when he first began to believe in God. 'I don't know,' he said. 'I've always known he exists.'"[13]

If faith is a shelter that nurtures, sustains, and protects us as we move through life, it is also a shelter that provides identity and support as we attempt to live our faith in the world. The tension present in the metaphor "making a home for faith" is one of affirming a life lived in the assurance of the presence of God while acknowledging the difficult challenge to live faithfully in the world in response to the waters of our baptism.[14]

Biblical scholar Walter Brueggemann wrote an article many years ago about confirmation in which he noted that being confirmed is an act of acknowledging that you are joining a story, joining a vision, and joining a crunch. Commenting on the notion of "crunch," Brueggemann said that "the life of Christian faith is a life of profound bother. It is centered in the awareness that there is an incongruity between what is and what God has intended."[15]

Those who are committed to making a clearing for God, a home for faith, are making the affirmation that living a bothered life is important. Making a home for faith requires both the intention of space for God, for listening and responding, and for action. As Sharon Parks points out, "We grow . . . by letting go and holding on, leaving and staying, journeying and abiding. A good life is a balance of home and pilgrimage."[16] As children of God, it is essential to seek this balance as we live together in the shelter of God's arms and in the community we call church.

Expressions of Hope

Sandy Eisenberg Sasso has written a book for all God's children titled *God in Between* in which she describes people who lived in a town with no roads or windows. With no way to look out or beyond their village, they wondered about the existence of God. There were two people who had windows in their homes, however, and so these two—"The Ones Who Could See Out Windows"—were sent out in hopes that they would find evidence of God. When they returned without finding God, the people in the town decided there was no God. After their return, The Ones Who Could See Out Windows began helping the people in the town to build roads to connect their houses and windows so they could see outside of their homes. In this activity, they came to know that God was "in the between, in between us."[17]

To consider the shelter of the children of God as a mission of the church is certainly an activity of seeing God in between. It has its expressions both in individual and in communal activities. Baptism is a sacrament of welcome for all God's children. Reflecting on how God's children are sheltered both by faith and in communities of faith, the sharing of meals at home and the celebration of the sacrament of the Lord's Table are visible expressions of hope.

Whether the place setting is for one or for many, the activity of setting tables of faith at home supports the continuing formation in faith of all of God's children. Life today for most families with children offers few times when they actually sit down to share a meal together. The lives of children and teenagers have become as busy as those of their parents. Some families are beginning to consider how to make a commitment to family time around the table.

Perhaps we could learn about the commitment to Sabbath time from our Jewish friends and neighbors. For Reform Jews, Friday evening is the beginning of Shabbat (Sabbath), and the observance and participation begin not at the congregation but at home with a meal. As candles are lit, blessings are said, and as families drink from the Kiddush cup and share the challah, they are reminded how Shabbat sanctifies time and helps them be aware of God's presence in their lives.

This Sabbath celebration moves from their dinner table at home to their congregation. An explicit connection is made between their faithful practices at home and their worship in the synagogue. Children grow up knowing that being Jewish means participating in this important ritual of faith. They grow up experiencing how they are sheltered in faith at home and at the synagogue.

This movement from prayers around the table at home to prayers at the synagogue represents an integration of faith and life that is essential for persons of faith. It is a ritual lost in many Christian families today. Growing in our understanding and experience of living in relationship with God who searches us and knows us, who calls us by name, requires time and space for Sabbath at home.

It is possible for children to grow up biblically illiterate in homes where Bibles abound but are rarely opened. Parents often think that church can provide the religious instruction for their child, and that is all they need. I think we are in danger of becoming a generation incapable of passing on the stories of our faith. "The face of our faith has become extremely impoverished. Instead of being rich banquets, feasts of faith and community, our tables of faith become barren with barely enough bread and water to satisfy, and we try to sustain ourselves on this meager diet."[18]

There are some creative expressions of hope visible around some tables in the homes of families today. Some mark the seasons of the church year with table runners in the traditional colors (blue for Advent, green for Ordinary Time, purple for Lent, white for Holy Days, and red for Pentecost). Special offering boxes for the One Great Hour of Sharing (Easter) and Pentecost help families to remember about sharing and the connection with the particular season.

Many congregations prepare meditation booklets for Advent and Lent. No matter whether you live alone or with others, using these resources for contemplation before eating is a way of personal and faithful preparation to listen for God. For families with children, using the ancient spiritual practice of the *Examen* is a way to connect faith and life and the sharing of a meal. It was written in 1541 by Ignatius of Loyola, who was instrumental in forming the Society of Jesus or the Jesuits, as a book of spiritual exercises. The *Examen* involves examining your life for the day. There are paired questions that can be asked in many different ways, for example:

- When did you receive God's love today? When did you give God's love today?
- What was something good that happened today? What was something bad that happened today?
- What were highs and lows of the day? Ignatius' version of this practice involves the consideration of "consolations" and

"desolations"—those times when God's spirit is enlivened and those times when it is stifled.[19]

- When did God seem most near to you today? When did God seem most far away?

Saturday evening as a family time before Sabbath might be a time for a spiritual practice that would help make the connection between the tables of faith at home and the gathering of the faith community on Sunday morning. A thoughtful way to mark the connection between the table at home and the Table of the Lord's Supper when it is celebrated at church helps children grow in their understanding of this special meal.

We move from our individual tables of faith to the joyous feast of the people of God, the celebration of the Eucharist where Jesus Christ is the host. The sacrament of baptism that was discussed in chapter one has a ritual movement from focus on the individual in the act of baptism to the welcome by the community to the newest one in their midst. The sacrament of the Lord's Supper moves from a communal celebration to individual expression as people leave the Table and move into the world. This sacrament represents a commitment of individual faith and communal sharing.

For this sacrament to really be an expression of hope for sheltering faith for the children of God, two things are required. First, there must be a renewed commitment to teaching and learning about the sacrament. Presbyterian congregations are no longer populated by a majority of persons who have grown up in this faith tradition. Gathered around the Table for this sacrament today are Catholics, Methodists, Pentecostals, Baptists, Lutherans, and persons who grew up with no faith tradition. Each adult brings with them their own understandings and practices of the sacrament.

Opportunities for adults to study the biblical background and theological meanings of the sacrament are important for congregations today. The liturgy that includes the Great Prayer of Thanksgiving provides opportunities for thanksgiving, remembrance, invoking God's Spirit, communion with the faithful gathered together in worship, and moving out into the world as God's faithful disciples. "The very celebration of the Eucharist is an instance of the Church's participation in God's mission to the world. This participation takes everyday form in the proclamation of the Gospel, service of the neighbor, and faithful presence in the world."[20]

Second, it is important for congregations to examine and reflect on their practices of the Sacrament of the Lord's Supper in light of

Presbyterian theology and polity. Though Christians share many common understandings and practices, there are some things unique to Presbyterians. We believe in an open Table, that anyone of any age who professes Jesus Christ as Lord and Savior is welcome at the Table. We welcome baptized children to the Lord's Table and believe that children who grow up sharing this meal within the faith community know in experiential ways that God's shelter of church welcomes them. In fact, the *Book of Order* spells out that no one should be excluded from the Table "because or race, sex, age, economic status, social class, handicapping condition, difference of culture or language, or any barrier created by human injustice."[21]

In writing about the relationship between the two sacraments, Catherine Gunsalus González has said:

> Baptism points to our participation in the death and resurrection of Jesus. So also does communion. . . . If baptism is the engrafting into Christ, the Lord's Supper is the continuous nourishment from the root that any graft needs if it is to stay alive. Jesus is the vine, and we are the branches. Baptism is the sign and seal of the beginning of our new life in Christ. Communion is the seal of the feeding of that new life.[22]

Given this theology and polity, it is hard to imagine why the shelter of faith offered by communing with Christians at the Lord's Table is denied to children and youth because church school is held the same time as worship. Such a model of religious education and practice of worship is spiritually impoverishing for children and youth and their teachers. It also means that the community of God's children gathered for worship is broken with their absence.

This statement about the sacrament from *A Declaration of Faith* makes clear the connections between our faith and our life in the world.

> We believe that at the Lord's Supper
> the community of believers is renewed
> by the memory of Christ's life and death,
> by his real presence in the power of the Holy Spirit,
> and by the promise of his coming again.
> Christ makes himself known to us in the breaking of bread. . . .

Reunited around one loaf and one cup,

we receive strength and courage

to continue our pilgrimage with God in the world.[23]

Congregations who welcome children and youth to the Lord's Table in the same ways that they joyously welcome and affirm their baptism are vivid expressions of hope for the church and the world. Children who grow in faith within the shelter of a loving congregation know how to take communion. They know the words to say when passing the bread, "This is the body of Christ" or "This is the bread of life." They know when passing the cup to say, "This is the blood of Christ" or "This is the cup or salvation."

A congregation I know had the story of Ruth and Naomi as a curricular theme for the church school. As a part of this fall focus, the sixth graders made bread to use for World Communion Sunday in October. They were also invited to serve communion with a parent on that Sunday. When I met with them for training about serving communion I asked them if they knew the words to use at the end of each pew. They were polite in their response of "Yes, of course we do," and they immediately repeated the words used in their congregation. I watched as young adolescents came forward with a family member to serve the congregation. It is in experiences like this that we fulfill our baptismal promises to welcome children both to the Christian faith and to its expression in the shelter of a faithful congregation.

Shaping Faith and Faithfulness

There is a definite liturgical rhythm that moves with us from our tables at home to the communion table. At both of these tables we remember family stories, we give thanks for the gift of food that nourishes our bodies, and we remember and give thanks for friends and family members who nourish our souls. At both tables we claim God's presence and we share a meal. In all of these moments of sharing at a table we are proclaiming our faith, saying who we are as Christians, and working with God to form the world as a place of love, shalom, and justice for all. These table activities have mysterious power both to form and to transform us.

It is always amazing how at communion there is enough bread, in fact, more than enough bread to share. I am also moved by visible rituals that move us from the table where we are fed to the tables we share in the world. I have been at Presbytery gatherings where small loaves of wrapped bread baked by an organization that hires the homeless are sent home, one for a representative from each congregation in the Presbytery. Attached to the loaf is the name of a sister church for whom you are to pray.

Baskets containing bread and a small cup sit on the communion table as a visible reminder of the sacrament being celebrated with those who are sick or unable to be in worship. Usually adults take this meal to shut-ins. What if kids were invited to go along with the adults? What if youth were invited to share the Eucharist with a shut-in and stay for a meal with them as a part of their confirmation education program?

Some congregations have a Loaf Ministry. On communion Sunday, the first of each month, loaves of bread baked by church members are taken to people who have visited the congregation during the last month.

Extra bread is baked for communion. It is shared with the shelter guests who gather for a meal on Sunday evening. Around tables, blessings are said, bread is broken. And we recall the words of invitation to the table:

> According to Luke,
>
> when our risen Lord was at table with his disciples,
>
> he took the bread, and blessed and broke it, and gave it to them.
>
> Then their eyes were opened
>
> and they recognized him.[24]

World Communion Sunday reminds us that Christians all over the world come to a common table. Breads of the world—pitas, flat breads, tortillas, loaves of all kinds, and rice cakes—fill a plate on World Communion Sunday to remind us we are connected across cultures and traditions in our common affirmation that Jesus is Lord!

Frederick Buechner, author and Presbyterian pastor, has eloquently written about home in, *The Longing for Home*. He speaks a word of woe to us,

> If we forget the homeless ones who have no vote, no power, nobody to lobby for them, and who might as well have no faces even, the way we try to avoid the troubling sight of them in the streets of the cities where they roam like stray cats. And as we listen each night to the news of what happened in our lives that day, woe to us too if we forget our own homelessness. . . . To be really at home is to be

really at peace, and our lives are so intricately interwoven that there can be no real peace for any of us until there is real peace for all of us. That is the truth that underlies not just the news of the world but the news of every one of our own days.[25]

Faith in God is truly a shelter that never collapses. Buechner reminds us of our connection with all humankind. In similar fashion, *A Declaration of Faith* reminds us: "We may misuse our freedom and deny our responsibility by trying to live without God and other people or against God and other people. Yet we are still bound to them for our life and well-being, and intended for free and responsible fellowship with them."[26]

Being a part of a faith community means that we engage in sheltering activities in mission in God's world together. Together we are interwoven and we weave a tapestry of faith that supports our faithful living in the world. Thanks be to God for sheltering arms of faith and love.

Notes

1. *A Brief Statement of Faith*, lines 49–51.
2. Morton Kelsey, *The Drama of Christmas: Getting Christ in Our Lives* (Louisville: Westminster John Knox Press, 1994).
3. *A Brief Statement of Faith*, lines 7–18.
4. *A Declaration of Faith*, chapter 2, section 4.
5. Sharon Daloz Parks, "Home and Pilgrimage: Companion Metaphors for Personal and Social Transformation," *Soundings* 72 (1989), 304.
6. Mary Pipher, *The Shelter of Each Other: Rebuilding Our Families* (New York: Putnam Publishing Co., 1996), 239.
7. Ibid., 240.
8. Ibid., 244.
9. This is a concept I have written about in *Making a Home for Faith: Nurturing the Spiritual Life of Your Children* (Cleveland: United Church Press, 2000).
10. Dana Tierney, "Coveting Luke's Faith," *New York Times*, January 11, 2004.
11. Ibid.
12. Ibid.
13. Ibid.
14. Elizabeth F. Caldwell, *Making a Home for Faith* (Cleveland: United Church Press, 2000), 6.
15. Walter Brueggemann, "Confirmation: Joining a Special Story," *Colloquy* (1974): 9.
16. Laurent A. Parks Daloz, Cheryl H. Keen, James P. Keen, and Sharon Daloz Parks *Common Fire: Lives of Commitment in a Complex World* (Boston: Beacon Press, 1996), 31.
17. Sandy Eisenberg Sasso, *God in Between* (Woodstock, VT: Jewish Lights Publishing, 1998).

18. Caldwell, 7.
19. Tony Jones, *Soul Shaper: Exploring Spirituality and Contemplative Practices in Youth Ministry* (El Cajon, CA: Youth Specialties, 2003), 104.
20. *Baptism, Eucharist, and Ministry*, Faith and Order Paper no. 111, (Geneva: World Council of Churches, 1982), 20.
21. *Book of Order*, W-2.4006.
22. Catherine Gunsalus González, *A Theology of the Lord's Supper* (Louisville: Presbyterian Church (U.S.A.), 1981), 13.
23. *A Declaration of Faith*, chapter 6, section 5.
24. *Book of Common Worship*, 68.
25. Frederick Buechner, *The Longing for Home* (San Francisco: Harper, 1996), 140.
26. *A Declaration of Faith*, chapter 2, section 4.

Questions for Reflection and Discussion

1. Caldwell asks the question, "Can we speak of the church as a shelter or even of faith as a shelter for persons who are formed in faith?" In what ways has the church been a shelter for you?

2. Read historical documents of the church (newsletters, bulletins, session minutes) from the last ten to twenty years. What do you learn about the church's commitment to being a shelter?

3. To whom did Jesus offer shelter? Recall stories from the Gospels of persons, named and unnamed, whom Jesus welcomed.

4. In what ways is your congregation serving as a shelter for those whom Jesus welcomed?

5. What clearing do you make for God in your life?

6. Consider Pipher's list of things that shelter families: time, places, interests, celebrations, connecting rituals, and stories and metaphors. Give examples for each of these things in relation to the life of your congregation.

7. In what ways has your congregation supported you in your life of faith, been a shelter for you? In what ways has your congregation challenged your life of faith?

8. Do you agree or disagree with Brueggemann's statement that joining the church is a crunch because "the life of Christian faith is a life of profound bother." Why?

9. What commitments to observing Sabbath are important for you? For your family?

10. Some creative expressions of hope visible around tables in the homes of Christian families today are described. What other spiritual practices are important to you? To your family?

11. Discuss your congregation's celebration of the Lord's Supper. Who is welcome at the Table? What opportunities to learn about this sacrament are given to children, adults, and families?

12. What new ideas for celebrating the Lord's Supper did you learn in this chapter?

Nurture

3

In 1861, Horace Bushnell wrote *Christian Nurture*, an important book by a prominent leader in the field of religious education. His concern was over how we are raised and how we grow in the life of the Christian faith. In response to those who believed that children must be evangelized, redeemed from the sin in which they were born, and led to make a profession of faith at a very young age, Bushnell wrote these timeless words:

> What is the true idea of Christian education? . . . That the child is to grow up a Christian, and never know himself as being otherwise. In other words, the aim, effort, and expectation should be, not, as is commonly assumed, that the child is to grow up in sin, to be converted after [she] comes to a mature age; but that [she] is to open on the world as one that is spiritually renewed, not remembering the time when [she] went through a technical experience, but seeming rather to have loved what is good from [her] earliest year.[1]

Dictionaries define nurture in two ways, as that which gives sustenance or nourishment and the activity of training and raising. These understandings are explicit in Bushnell's definition. Notice the connection he makes between growing up as a Christian and the activity of being "open on the world as one that is spiritually renewed."

Perhaps the authors of the Great Ends of the Church were familiar with Bushnell's writing because they included the nurture of the children of God as a priority for the church's mission. Christian education is a way we would speak today of this activity of nurturing God's children of all ages in the life of the Christian faith.

Commitment to Christian nurture has been a major priority for the Presbyterian Church throughout its history in its various configurations.

The *Book of Order* makes this clear in the section on The Church and Its Mission, in which we read that as the church, we are called to live out our love for Jesus Christ by "sharing in worship, fellowship, and nurture, practicing a deepened life of prayer and service under the guidance of the Holy Spirit."[2]

The responsibility of this work of mission is given to the session, which has the responsibility and the power to:

> provide for the growth of its members and for their equipment for ministry through personal and pastoral care, educational programs including the church school, sharing in fellowship and mutual support, and opportunities for witness and service in the world; to develop and supervise the church school and the educational program of the church . . .[3]

In addition to duties of budget, stewardship, mission, and administration, the officers of the congregation are expected "to lead the congregation continually to discover what God is doing in the world and to plan for change, renewal, and reformation under the Word of God."[4] Perhaps this is a good example of what Bushnell was referring to when he wrote that a child "is to open on the world as one that is spiritually renewed." A congregation that is providing nurture for all of God's children of every age is committed to living with the Word of God in order to discover in new ways "what God is doing in the world and to plan for change, renewal, and reformation." This is Christian nurture.

Biblical Images

This notion of self in relation to God as a constant, nurturing presence, one that does not need a dramatic introduction, is also a concept at the heart of the "Great Commandment" or the *Shema* in Deuteronomy 6:4–9.

> The LORD is our God, the LORD alone. You shall love the LORD your God with all your heart, and with all your soul, and with all your might. Keep these words that I am commanding you today in your heart. Recite them to your children and talk about them when you are at home and when you are away, when you lie down and when you rise. Bind them as a sign on your hand, fix them as an emblem

on your forehead, and write them on the doorposts of your house and on your gates.

Recall a moment in your life when you experienced the presence of God. Remember a time when a connection was made for you between God's Word and your life. This kind of connection is made explicit in Deuteronomy 6:4–9. In his commentary on Deuteronomy, Patrick D. Miller has said that chapters five through eleven in Deuteronomy form the centerpiece of the book. These chapters are "the most important words for those who would cross the border to live as God's people in the place and in the way that God has set for them."[5]

I am intrigued with Miller's comment about the importance of these words to the faithful follower of God to describe faithful living "in the place and in the way" that God has shown. I find the image of crossing a border particularly noteworthy. The Hebrew people were on a journey with God. The Bible tells the story of their wanderings, their confusion, their certainties, and their doubts. In all this, God attempted to show them in burning bushes, on clay tablets, through parting waters and stones placed beside waters, through faithful leaders and a feast of manna in the wilderness, that God was always faithful, always loving, always present.

The Bible is truly the story of God's love of humankind, God's seeking out the creation in a nurturing relationship of steadfast love. The life of the Hebrew people, not unlike ours today, was a series of crossing borders as they attempted to live in faithfulness to God. Crossing borders implies movement, change, and journeys, all strong images for the life of faith.

The *Shema*, or the Great Commandment as it is called, is a pivotal piece for the rest of Deuteronomy, because of its location, immediately after the Ten Commandments, and because of its placement as a bridge between the Ten Commandments and the explanation of the statutes and ordinances that follow in Deuteronomy 12—26. This statement of faith identifies the relationship between God and God's people and names for the people their identity as God's own.

It begins with a claim, not a demand: "Hear O Israel: The LORD is our God, the LORD alone." The passage makes a clear argument for a unity of thinking, believing, and acting. You shall love the Lord your God with all your mind, with all your strength, and with all your being.

We cross a lot of borders each day of our lives as we leave our homes for our work and as we feed children and send them off to school with hugs and kisses and a backpack. We cross borders as we share coffee and conversation with a neighbor or co-worker who is Jewish or Catholic or Muslim. The borders of our life are shaken a bit as we read and see the news of war and famine, of the continuing crisis of AIDS in Africa, of the increasing and seemingly never-ending violence of neighbor against neighbor in the Middle East, or of neighborhoods and schools in this country that are not safe places for children and families.

And as we cross these daily borders, we have this commandment in our memory bank: "You shall love the Lord your God with all your heart, and with all your soul, and with all your might." This is such a deceptively simple thing to remember! Yes, I love God with all my being—with my heart, with all my strength, even with all my might. Then I look at my life, for the evidence of that love.

And then Jesus, in quoting this scripture, adds a second commandment: "You shall love your neighbor as yourself" (Matt. 22:39). Living amid the diversity of our world requires that we speak and live faithfully, loving God with our whole being and loving God by the ways in which we love our neighbor. These two texts are the beginning, the foundation for our understanding of what it means to be nurtured in a life of faith.

A Brief Statement of Faith provides some clues about the role of the Spirit of God in nurturing our lives of faith.

> We trust in God the Holy Spirit,
> > everywhere the giver and renewer of life.
> > The Spirit justifies us by grace through faith,
> > > sets us free to accept ourselves and to love God and
> > > > neighbor,
> > > and binds us together with all believers
> > > in the one body of Christ, the Church.
> > The same Spirit
> > > who inspired the prophets and apostles
> > > rules our faith and life in Christ through Scripture,
> > > engages us through the Word proclaimed,
> > > claims us in the waters of baptism,
> > > feeds us with the bread of life and the cup of salvation,
> > > and calls women and men to all ministries of the Church.[6]

Notice the verbs used to describe the work of God's Spirit: justifies us by grace, sets us free, binds us together, rules our faith and life, engages, claims, feeds, and calls. This is Christian nurture.

The other contemporary confession we have been using in this book, *A Declaration of Faith*, has commented on the importance of teaching in the church as an activity that "prepares people to hear the Word of God and enables them to reflect and act on it."[7] Chapter Nine of this confession focuses on Christian discipleship and says that "Christ calls us to be disciples . . . to live in disciplined freedom, . . . to live in the presence of God, . . . to live for our neighbors, . . . to pilgrimage toward the kingdom." In mission, "God sends the church into the world, to proclaim the gospel, to strive for justice, to exercise compassion, to work for peace."[8]

To be Christ's disciples, to be God's living presence in the world, we must make the activity of nurturing God's children in the life of faith a congregational priority. In what ways is your congregation preparing people to hear the Word of God? In what ways is your congregation supporting people in their personal and communal activities of reflecting and acting upon God's Word in God's world?

The words of the *Shema* remind us to keep God's words in our hearts. This spiritual nurturing supports our living in the world. And Jesus' teaching calls us to remember that the love we have received from God is to be shared with our neighbors.

Challenging Possibilities

Presbyterian pastor Jim Kitchens has written about the new context for ministry, which he characterizes as post-modern, post-Christian, and post-denominational. Old assumptions that congregations are made up of people raised within a faith tradition are no longer valid. Kitchens believes that

> merely teaching content *about* the faith, the reigning model of Christian education up until the last generation, isn't going to do the job. Rather, you will need to introduce people to the basic narrative of scripture, the spiritual disciplines of prayer and worship, and the shape of Christian living. Formation will need to replace education as our model of Christian nurture.[9]

What are the purposes for which we are educating in faith? What are our hopes for a child who moves through preschool, elementary, and youth? What do we want them to know, to value, and to experience of the Christian faith? And what about adults of all ages? What content, settings, and approaches to teaching and learning will best nurture their lives of faith? Questions such as these challenge congregations to consider the possibilities for the Christian nurture of all of God's children. Nurture or Christian Education Committees who are responsible for settings and content of religious education often focus most of their energy on keeping the church school functioning—finding teachers, writing or selecting curriculum, and planning for other times when the faith community comes together for Christian nurture.

Contemplation is equally important, both for evaluation and for visioning, imagining what might be, and where the greatest needs for spiritual nurture are in the congregation. This kind of time provides the opportunity to rethink congregational commitments and models of Christian education or Christian formation.

Consider for a moment your own definition about the purpose of Christian nurture in the congregation. Then scan the following definitions that are written by historic and contemporary leaders in the field of religious education. As you read, use these icons to notate your own thoughts or reflections as you relate these definitions to your congregation's settings for Christian nurture.

? —Places where you have questions
* —Places where you are in agreement
@ —Places that connect you to a thought, a conversation, an idea
! —Places where there is something you want to remember

Defining Christian Education

1. "We teach so that through our teaching God may work in the hearts of those whom we teach to make of them disciples wholly committed to his gospel, with an understanding of it, and with a personal faith that will enable them to bear convincing witness to it in word and action in the midst of an unbelieving world. . . . We teach young children and youths and adults that by the grace of God they may grow up into the full life and faith of his Church, and may find their life's fulfillment in being members of the very body of Christ and sharers in his mission."[10]

2. "Christian Education is the believing community at work helping people listen and look in order that by God's grace they may hear and see and so be helped to know the hope to which they are called by God in Jesus Christ."[11]

3. "The aim of education is that we may become persons who see things as they are and who come to grips with life." The work of the teaching ministry of the church is to deliver the gospel message, help people prepare for response to it, "show them how to respond, [and] help them to see and work out the fullness of its implications."[12]

4. "My thesis is that faith is communicated by a community of believers and that the meaning of faith is developed by its members out of their history, by their interaction with each other, and in relation to the events that take place in their lives."[13]

5. "Christian religious education is a political activity with pilgrims in time that deliberately and intentionally attends with them to the activity of God in our present, to the Story of the Christian faith community, and to the Vision of God's kingdom, the seeds of which are already among us."[14]

6. "[We need to help] persons develop beliefs which inform and reshape the cultures of church and society. Moreover, we need to be more deliberate in our approach to helping persons claim the Christian inheritance in such a way that they can come to know who they are and why they are. Teaching, then, as an intentional activity, may be employed as an instrument for use by the church in helping persons find meaning in a chaotic world."[15]

7. "Christian Education is a process of opening the channels of grace so that women and men might know and accept their Lord. . . . This process involved celebration of the biblical story through participation in a witnessing and serving Christian community."[16]

8. "Christian education involves those tasks and expressions of ministry that enable people: (1) to learn the Christian story—both ancient and present; (2) to develop the skills they need to act out their faith; . . . (3) to reflect on that story in order to live self-aware to its truth; [and] (4) to nurture the sensitivities they need to live together as a covenant community."[17]

9. "The key to adult religious education is to be found in *making connections*—within our own selves, with persons in our own faith communities, among laity and professional church staff, between professional educators and pastors, with those in our own and other Christian traditions, between Christians and Jews, with persons of other faith traditions (both Eastern and Western world religions and the religions of indigenous peoples), and with all persons of good will who are committed to working toward a world that is justice-producing and life-sustaining for the planet and every being on it. Sculpting meaning and nourishing souls have much to do with forming connections."[18]

10. "The education of Christians requires participation in the struggle to discern life in light of the incarnation of God, by remembering, loving, telling, and retelling life's story in light of God. . . . Working to enhance the church as an environment of Christian learning is central to the task of Christian education. Christian education is about forming faith, the basic meaning—perspectives through which a person views reality. Faith formation means that the perspectives of Christian faith become a lens through which persons view the world."[19]

11. "The congregation is the context, and its mission—to praise God and serve neighbors—the impetus for Christian religious education. The purpose of church education flows out of these two statements. It is to 'build up' or construct communities of faith to praise God and serve neighbors for the sake of the 'emancipatory transformation of the world.'"[20]

12. In commenting on the purpose of Christian education from the perspective of why people participate, one educator has said "Many participants seek spiritual and educational enrichment through their dialogue with the Bible and one another. . . . Some seek to validate ways they have handled life struggles or how they are now living out the intricate details of their lives. Some look for specific answers to issues and questions arising from dire life circumstances. They seek freedom from these circumstances and pathways to a better and more meaningful life. . . . [People] enter Christian education contexts at different junctures in their lives for different reasons."[21]

13. "[Preparation] to live with a face of faith in the world . . . requires that adult Christians make intentional commitments

to nurturing their faith, both individually and communally. Establishing regular patterns of spiritual formation—habits of mind and heart—has the power to feed hungry souls and form a face of faith that can meet the world with all of its demands and challenges."[22]

14. "Growth in the life of faith also involves a lifelong, continuing process of encountering and entering into the inexhaustible richness of the mystery of God and of God's love, ever more deeply and profoundly. Just as the process of knowing a person is never finished or exhausted, so too the dynamic of uncovering the riches of God's grace and promises is unlimited. Thus we grow in the life of faith as we hear more and more of the good news of the living gospel, understand and appropriate more profoundly its unceasingly expanding meaning and significance, and dwell ever more fully on the presence of God with us."[23]

15. "Christian formation is a process as old as the church itself. It is the process of helping a person who may initially be drawn only to one aspect of Christian life (for example, those young parents' interest in their children's moral education) discover the depth of life and the full richness of faith the tradition offers. Formation is as much about developing Christian disciplines and practices as it is about gaining knowledge about the Christian tradition."[24]

There are some common threads running through these definitions. The connection of nurture to the context of the congregation affirms the communal nature of the life of faith. We are the body of Christ and the role of the community in supporting and challenging our lives of faith is essential for growth.

Several of the definitions point to the importance of Christian nurture or education in helping individuals name and appropriate responses as they "discern life" in light of God's incarnating work. "Making connections," a "face of faith," a "lens" through which to view the world are terms used by several to describe the role of the Christian in interpreting Scripture and living in response to God's love.

Anne Streaty Wimberly refers to the variety of reasons why adults participate in Christian education contexts. For some, it is a spiritual or Sabbath practice, "what I or my family do on Sunday." Others are drawn to Christian education programs because of a title of a particular program, class, or retreat.

Jim Kitchens is correct about the need for educational and pastoral leaders in the church to help persons discover the "depth of life and the full richness of faith" that our tradition has to offer.

Congregational programs of Christian nurture offer challenging possibilities for evaluation and reflection on the needs of the community for Christian formation.

Expressions of Hope

Maria Harris has called the activity of teaching a "profound vocation" and "an act of religious imagination."[25] In defining religious imagination she uses the terms contemplative, ascetic, creative, and sacramental. Before her retirement, Maria was committed to helping teachers consider the ways they could work out of their own imaginations.

She developed five criteria that she considered to be "paths to take or moments in which to dwell." She believed that teachers who are engaged in self-reflection and continued learning will Take Steps, Take Care, Take Form, Take Time, and Take Risks. I believe these five criteria offer expressions of hope for the church as it considers its nurturing role.

Craig Dykstra's definition used earlier in this chapter provides a helpful context for thinking imaginatively about the ways we take steps, care, form, time, and risks in the Christian nurture of all God's children.

> Growth in the life of faith also involves a lifelong, continuing process of encountering and entering into the inexhaustible richness of the mystery of God and of God's love, ever more deeply and profoundly. Just as the process of knowing a person is never finished or exhausted, so too the dynamic of uncovering the riches of God's grace and promises is unlimited. Thus we grow in the life of faith as we hear more and more of the good news of the living gospel, understand and appropriate more profoundly its unceasingly expanding meaning and significance, and dwell ever more fully on the presence of God with us.[26]

Taking Steps

The church is one of the few places in the culture where people come together in community across the life span. This inclusive hospitality is one of the greatest and yet most challenging gifts we face in living together in the community of faith. From the beginning of life when a child is born or adopted by a family until the last breaths taken, we believe that all are welcome in God's family. We welcome infants with the waters of baptism and ask questions of the congregation about their commitment to nurture this child in the life of the Christian faith.

Dykstra has said that growth in the life of faith "involves a lifelong, continuing process of encountering and entering into the inexhaustible richness of the mystery of God and of God's love, ever more deeply and profoundly."[27] The many settings that we are able to provide require that we take two very important steps.

First, we must take steps to evaluate the intentional or formal ways that people are nurtured in the life of faith. What models are at work in your congregation? For other congregations, the church school hour on Sunday morning is a time when there are learning opportunities for all ages prior to or following worship where all are welcome. For many congregations, a one-hour model means that adults can go to worship while children and youth are in church school. Sadly, this model means that children are excluded from the worshiping community, and adults are not expected to participate in learning opportunities.

A growing group of churches have evaluated their model of Christian education with children and decided to change to the rotation model in which elementary age children focus on fewer Biblical stories but engage with them more fully through art, music, drama, video, and computers.[28] This model is exciting and engaging for both learners and teachers.

Second, we must take steps to help people make connections between the biblical text, their lives, and the world. One way to do that is to ensure that all voices are heard, that everyone participates, that space and time are available for all. Taking steps to evaluate programs and settings for Christian nurture gives a congregation the opportunity to identify goals and purposes of Christian education.

- By the time a child has moved out of elementary grades, what Biblical stories or themes will they have had the chance to study?
- What experiences of mission will youth have had the chance to participate in before they graduate from high school?

- What opportunities for hearing and reflecting on biblical text and making connections with their own lives of faith are being offered for adults in the congregation?

Taking Care

Churches that are committed to the activity of Christian nurture as an important mission of the church take care of educational leaders and teachers. Unfortunately, the commitment to teaching in the church school has become a low priority in many congregations. It has been abandoned by the congregation as a communal commitment made public at a baptism and left to parents of children. Like students graduating from high school, many adults believe that they too graduate from the nurturing responsibilities for active involvement in church education, either as a participant or as a leader or teacher.

For Maria Harris, taking care as a teacher means that we have reverence and respect for ourselves as well as for the learners and the content. Consider the formal settings where teaching and learning take place in your congregation: church school on Sunday; midweek educational programs for children, youth, and adults; youth group gatherings; women's and men's midweek Bible study or prayer groups; and new member classes.

It is time to take care in the nurture and support of teachers and leaders of these groups. Who is responsible for inviting them to share their gifts of teaching with the congregation? In what ways are their gifts and talents recognized and valued by the congregation? The writer of the latter part of Isaiah has said, "The Lord God has given me the tongue of a teacher, that I may know how to sustain the weary with a word" (Isa. 50:4). It is time to share the secret that one excellent way to know more about the Bible is to take on a role in teaching.

It is time to take care in finding teachers for the variety of settings of teaching and learning that congregations believe are important to offer. It is time to take care in saying that teaching in the church school is a spiritual gift. It is time to honor those who make this commitment to teach by encouraging them to do this one thing well and not expect them to do ten other jobs in the church. In writing about the care that teachers take, educator Parker Palmer has said:

I believe that knowing, teaching, and learning are grounded in sacred soil and that renewing my vocation as a teacher requires cultivating a sense of the sacred. . . . In a world stripped of the sacred, the inner landscape holds no mystery, for it has no variety. . . . In a sacred landscape, with its complexities and convolutions, surprise is a constant companion: it lies just around the bend or hidden in the next valley, and though it sometimes startles us, it often brings delight."[29]

Taking Form

Adult education is one area of the church's work in Christian nurture that needs both new energy and commitments. Larger congregations, recognizing the variety of faith traditions and life experiences represented in adults across the life span, are developing models of adult religious education with titles such as the Academy of Faith and Life.[30] This model includes a variety of short-term (six- to eight-week) classes that require registration and sometimes small fees. Classes are offered in fall, winter, and spring terms, much like the format of higher education. Many congregations have classes formed around particular curriculum or teachers.

Some new church developments that focus on ministry with young adults use a variety of contexts for Christian formation. Coffee shops and restaurants, and even bars, become a setting for conversation and discussion.

Recall another part of Dykstra's definition: "Just as the process of knowing a person is never finished or exhausted, so too the dynamic of uncovering the riches of God's grace and promises is unlimited."[31] Earlier in this chapter, Jim Kitchens suggested that formation needs to become our model of Christian nurture.

Taking form means that adult education makes formation of persons a priority for Christian nurture. It means that time is taken in settings of adult education for persons to become a faithful community of learners. Parker Palmer has described six paradoxical tensions that he seeks to build into a teaching and learning space. I find these helpful in talking with adult learners about norms for learning, norms that support the form for our teaching. Consider these six tensions:[32]

1. **The space should be bounded and open.** We create boundaries in our teaching through our use of questions and texts, through those things that help everyone focus on the topic. At the same time, we are open to discovery of the "a-has!" that come with real learning.[32]
2. **The space should be hospitable and "charged."** The environment of teaching should be inviting, open, and safe. The space must be a place of trust, yet also a place of challenge and risk taking.

3. **The space should invite the voice of the individual and the voice of the group.** The space to hear individual voices is also a place larger than individual expression, a place where the voice of the group is heard, gathered, amplified so the group can affirm, question, challenge, and correct the voice of the individual.

4. **The space should honor the "little" stories of the students and the "big" stories of the disciplines and tradition.** The space should accommodate the hearing of individual stories as well as the larger stories from our discipline, which are "universal in scope and archetypal in depth."

5. **The space should support solitude and surround it with the resources of community.** What is the compatibility of the individual and the group? "In a community that respects the mystery of the soul, we help each other remove impediments to discernment."

6. **The space should welcome both silence and speech.** We educate with both silence and speech—speech to voice what we know and experience; silence to reflect on what we have said and heard.

Consider these six tensions as you reflect on your own teaching, which side of the tension is easier for you to build into a session? Which is harder? Why?

Taking Time

For imagination to emerge, Harris has said, "Take time. For revelation is gradual unfolding in the sun, inevitably, necessarily, as tomcats stretch; revelation is closely related to human birth and does not happen except in its own time; revelation cannot be guaranteed; revelation must be waited upon."[33]

We live in a culture where time has become one of the most precious things we possess. For many, there never seems to be enough time to get everything done. People are spending longer hours at work, even bringing work home. Technology means we are never far away from the demands of our work. We live in a world of time governed by *chronos*, speed, change, and over-scheduled lives lived by the clock. Culturally we are caught in a difficult tension. *Chronos* time values speed and not having to wait for anything. We grow impatient when the Internet connection slows down for even a few seconds. If you hesitate when the traffic light turns green, car horns begin to blow.

And yet our life of faith is nurtured by an understanding of time that is *kairos*, Sabbath time, time that is God-given. If lives are lived by the clock, what happens to attunement to *kairos* time, being with God?

It is a matter of prioritizing our time. Spirituality is being attuned to the mystery and wonder of God's presence in our lives.

What does time have to do with nurturing God's children in the life of the Christian faith? Consider how we are stewards of our time and consider again Dykstra's definition: "Thus we grow in the life of faith as we hear more and more of the good news of the living gospel, understand and appropriate more profoundly its unceasingly expanding meaning and significance, and dwell ever more fully on the presence of God with us."[34]

The formational activity of growing in the life of faith is nurtured and sustained by hearing, understanding, appropriating, and dwelling. The last part of this statement about dwelling "ever more fully on the presence of God with us" requires a commitment to *kairos* or Sabbath time.

Taking Risks

Maria Harris believes that "risk-takers are the ones who have contributed most to human re-creation and transformation."[35] Risk, she believes, is called for "when the powers . . . to be discovered and claimed are not only the powers to receive and to love, but also the powers to rebel, to resist, and to reform."[36] Learning is really beyond our control. Teaching and learning in congregational settings are about important matters of the soul and time. The process is both sacred and perilous because of its importance. What is at risk in learning, which shapes life and belief?

Learning can be the most exciting, challenging, and life-changing experience—or it can be dull and boring. Those who are responsible for educational leadership in the church need to spend time observing education in public schools, colleges, and universities.

- How are methods of teaching and learning and the forming of learning communities being shaped by the teacher?
- How is technology changing both the setting for learning and the process of teaching and learning?
- What risks are educators taking in public education?
- What new things need to emerge in congregational settings of Christian education?
- In what ways do the settings for Christian education invite learners to use all of their imagination in learning a biblical story and connecting it with their lives of faith?
- What risks have you taken as a teacher? In what ways has risk contributed to your continuing growth as teacher?

I agree with Maria Harris and appreciate her challenge to nurture imagination by taking steps, taking form, taking time, taking care, and taking risks. I accepted her challenge as I redesigned a course on teaching methods that I was planning to teach at McCormick Theological Seminary. I took steps to redesign the course in a new form, deciding to take care and to take a risk in my teaching by taking time. I invited twenty-one adult learners representing at least eight faith traditions and five cultures—Korean, Puerto Rican, Sri Lankan, African American, and Caucasian—to think about their role as teachers by engaging in discussion about readings, teaching the class, and joining me in taking time at the end of each class for silence, meditation, and journaling.

I did not know what the reaction would be from graduate students whose lives are full of responsibilities for family, church, jobs, and class preparation. How would they react to silence? I knew I needed it. After I modeled it during the first class, they signed up to close class each week in whatever way they wanted—prayer, music, a reading, or journaling in silence. Once when I forgot to light the candle, they did it for me. Some journaled, some meditated, eyes were closed, eyes were open. In reflecting on this activity in a final paper, a student wrote:

> This time allowed space for reflection and integration of what I had received during each class. I did not write a journal; I instead practiced silence. Silence is very special to go deep into listening to God's voice. I liked the diversity of readings and prayers and how they were conducive to a wider appreciation of each moment, of each particular classmate, of how we as a group ventured into learning together. It also enforces the idea that spirituality and teaching are joined hand in hand and that we must always think about ways in which teaching is beneficial to the mind, but also to the soul.[37]

This is nurture, educating the mind while also tending to the soul.

Shaping Faith and Faithfulness

In *Growing Up Religious: Christians and Jews and Their Journeys of Faith*, Robert Wuthnow writes about the findings from interviews conducted with two hundred men and women over a three-year period. He was interested in knowing the ways in which spirituality is being refocused in our time. He discovered that growing up religious was strongly related to social relationships at home and at church. He speaks of "embedded practices," the everyday things that we remember as important. "Embedded practices are influential in religious development because they spin out webs of significance that richly connect people with the world around them."[38]

Getting ready to go to church as a family, meals shared together after church, and bedtime prayers are nurturing practices of faith that provide roots for spiritual formation. In contrast to the experiential nature of these activities stands the more formal nature of religious instruction.

> Influenced by the legacy of catechetical instruction, scholars
> have continued to assume that children are first and foremost
> mental machines. Incessantly curious, children presumably
> start asking questions about the nature of the universe at an
> early age, and if they are supplied with simple answers at
> the right moment, then they will progress through various
> stages of cognitive development until they achieve the
> sophistication of an adult understanding of faith.[39]

Wuthnow's research did not confirm this assumption. Rather, in listening to people talk about "growing up religious" they came to understand that "they assimilated religion more by osmosis than by instruction. . . . Spirituality also came to be understood as a way of life, and it did so because people grew up living it."[40]

Wuthnow's findings echo the earlier statement from Horace Bushnell about the experiential nature of Christian nurture. Growing in the life of Christian faith requires many nurturing contexts. In the church we offer intentional opportunities for learning and growth in our formation as Christians. Yet these formal settings, whether they are in the church or in places in the community, are not adequate in and of themselves for nurturing Christians. They need the partnership of the home. It is that topic which is the focus for the next chapter.

Notes

1. Horace Bushnell, *Christian Nurture*, reprinted from the 1861 edition published by Charles Scribner (Cleveland: The Pilgrim Press, 1994), 10.
2. *Book of Order*, G-3.0300.
3. Ibid., G-10.000–.0102.
4. Ibid.
5. Patrick D. Miller, *Deuteronomy: Interpretation; a Bible Commentary for Teaching and Preaching* (Louisville: Westminster John Knox Press, 1990), 65–66.

6. *A Brief Statement of Faith*, lines 52–64.
7. *A Declaration of Faith*, chapter 6, section 4.
8. Ibid., chapter 9, section 8.
9. Jim Kitchens, *The Postmodern Parish: New Ministry for a New Era* (New York: The Alban Institute, 2003), 28.
10. James D. Smart, *The Teaching Ministry of the Church: An Examination of the Basic Principles of Christian Education* (Philadelphia: The Westminster Press, 1954), 107.
11. Hulda Niebuhr, "Communicating the Gospel through Christian Education," *McCormick Speaking* (March, 1958), 13.
12. D. Campbell Wyckoff, *The Gospel and Christian Education: A Theory of Christian Education for Our Times* (Philadelphia: The Westminster Press, 1959), 54, 108.
13. C. Ellis Nelson, *Where Faith Begins* (Atlanta: John Knox Press, 1971), 10.
14. Thomas H. Groome, *Christian Religious Education: Sharing Our Story and Vision* (San Francisco: Harper & Row, 1980), 25.
15. Sara Little, *To Set One's Heart: Belief and Teaching in the Church* (Atlanta: John Knox Press, 1983), 5.
16. Letty M. Russell, "Changing My Mind about Religious Education," *Religious Education* 79: 1 (Winter 1984), 9–10.
17. Daniel Aleshire, "Finding Eagles in the Turkeys' Nest: Pastoral Theology and Christian Education," *Review and Expositor* 85 (1988): 701–702.
18. Linda J. Vogel, *Teaching and Learning in Communities of Faith: Empowering Adults through Religious Education* (San Francisco: Jossey-Bass, 1991), 179–180.
19. Jack Seymour, Margaret Ann Crain, and Joseph Crockett, *Educating Christians* (Nashville: Abingdon Press, 1993).
20. Charles R. Foster, *Educating Congregations: The Future of Christian Education* (Nashville: Abingdon Press, 1994), 13.
21. Anne Streaty Wimberly, *Soul Stories: African American Christian Education* (Nashville: Abingdon Press, 1994), 19.
22. Elizabeth F. Caldwell, "Religious Instruction: Homemaking," in *Mapping Christian Education: Approaches to Congregational Learning*, ed. Jack L. Seymour (Nashville: Abingdon Press, 1997), 87.
23. Craig R. Dykstra, *Growing in the Life of Faith: Education and Christian Practices* (Louisville: Geneva Press, 1999), 38.
24. Kitchens, 61.
25. Maria Harris, *Teaching and Religious Imagination: An Essay in the Theology of Teaching* (San Francisco: Harper & Row, 1987), 10, 181.
26. Dykstra, 38.
27. Ibid.
28. This model is described more fully in *Workshop Rotation* by Melissa Armstrong-Hansche and Neil MacQueen, Geneva, 2002. Two Web sites support this model: www.sundaysoftware.com and www.rotation.org.
29. Palmer, 111–112.
30. This is the name the Fourth Presbyterian Church in Chicago uses for its classes offered for adults.
31. Dykstra, 38.
32. Palmer, 74–77.
33. Harris, 172.

34. Dykstra, 38.
35. Harris, 178.
36. Ibid., 179.
37. Thanks to Noe Mojica, a Master of Divinity student at McCormick Theological Seminary, who shared these thoughts.
38. Robert Wuthnow, *Growing Up Religious: Christians and Jews and Their Journeys of Faith* (Boston: Beacon Press, 1999), xxxvi.
39. Ibid., xxxvi–xxxvii.
40. Ibid., xxxvii.
41. Kitchens, 28.

Questions for Reflection and Discussion

1. In what ways were you nurtured in faith when you were a child? In what ways did you "grow up religious," to use Wuthnow's phrase?

2. What is your response to Jim Kitchens' suggestion that "formation will need to replace education as our model of Christian nurture?"[41]

3. What opportunities for learning and experiencing the basics of scripture, prayer, worship, and ways to live faithfully in the world are offered in your congregation?

4. Where are people given opportunities to reflect on their living of the Christian life in the world?

5. If you were to write a definition of the purpose of Christian education or Christian nurture, what would you say? Compare your definition with those included in this chapter.

6. Read through the definitions. What questions and affirmations are raised for you in these statements? What common themes are apparent in these definitions?

7. In what ways is your congregation preparing people to hear the Word of God? In what ways is your congregation supporting people in their personal and communal activities of reflecting and acting upon God's Word in God's world?

8. What are the goals for your programs of Christian education with children, youth, and adults? By the time a child has moved out of the elementary grades, what biblical stories or themes will they have had the chance to study? What experiences of mission will youth have had the chance to participate in before they graduate from high school? What opportunities for hearing and reflecting on biblical text and making connections with

their own lives of faith are being offered for adults in the congregation?

9. What is your congregation's model of Christian nurture? Which of the definitions has the greatest connection to your model?

10. In what ways are teachers and educational leaders nurtured and supported?

11. In what ways is your congregation committed to the Christian nurture of all God's children in taking steps, care, form, time, and risk?

12. As you read over Parker Palmer's six paradoxical tensions, how might these be used when providing instruction on how to teach in educational settings in the church?

13. What opportunities for Christian formation are most needed for adults in your context?

Spiritual Fellowship

4

Midweek church suppers followed by classes for all ages, youth group gatherings, mission trips, meals shared around the table with guests from the homeless shelter, preschool children's morning play group— the list of gatherings of the church family is an endless variety of opportunities for spiritual fellowship. The children's choir goes to the retirement center to sing and visit with church members. Young adults gather for their book discussion in a neighborhood coffee shop. Women's groups gather for study and fellowship, choir members come together for practice, and a men's breakfast group gathers on a Saturday workday at the church. Someone has a death in the family, and church members begin coming by the house with platters of food and words of comfort and offerings of silent presence.

In a culture and a world that values individualism and individuation, we preach and teach a biblical theology of community, God's people gathered together. As we continue to create and expand technology for communication and entertainment, the church also attempts to market its message of its message of being a spiritual home.

Anne Lamott writes about the fellowship she found in St. Andrew's Presbyterian Church. In writing about why she makes her son go to church, she explains:

> The main reason is that I want to give him what I found in the world, which is to say a path and a little light to see by. Most of the people I know who have what I want—which is to say, purpose, heart, balance, gratitude, joy—are people with a deep sense of spirituality. They are people in community, who pray, or practice their faith; they are Buddhists, Jews, Christians—people banding together to work on themselves and for human rights. They follow a brighter light than theglimmer of their own candle; they are part of something beautiful. . . . Our funky little church is

filled with people who are working for peace and freedom, who are out there on the streets and inside praying, and they are home writing letters, and they are at the shelters with giant platters of food.

When I was at the end of my rope, the people at St. Andrews tied a knot in it for me and helped me hold on.[1]

For those who have experienced the kind of spiritual fellowship like the settings described above, they will recognize the ebb and flow of the life of Christians living together in the faith community. The church preaches and teaches an alternative to the self-made individualism so important in American culture. The congregation comes together, children of God of all ages, to learn, to worship, and to serve.

To speak of the spiritual fellowship of God's children is to recognize both its explicit and implicit expressions whenever the people of God gather. What does spiritual fellowship look like? Spiritual fellowship wears many hats. It is certainly represented in the gatherings of women's groups for Bible study, in prayer and community, in the prayers before meals shared with shelter guests, and in the blessings at the end of a child's church school class. Spiritual fellowship is more implicitly present in conversations over coffee or tea before or after church. Spiritual fellowship includes all the ways that Christians are involved in the daily practices of their faith.

In this chapter I will examine several definitions of spirituality and consider activities of spiritual practice that nurture a life of faith and sustain and enrich the spiritual fellowship of God's people gathered in a congregation. I will also review selected current literature in the area of spiritual practices.

The Great Ends of the Church are missional statements meant to guide us as a denomination. As we think about spiritual fellowship, it becomes apparent that if we are to be God's faithful witnesses in the world, then it is essential to be prepared for this call and vocation. Attending to and taking care of our spiritual selves enables our work in mission in God's world. Spiritual fellowship has both communal and individual priorities.

Biblical Images

The book of Acts provides insight into the life of the earliest Christians after the ascension of Jesus. It must have been a rather frightening time for them. Their teacher and leader, Jesus, was no longer physically present with them. He left with a promise that the Holy Spirit would be with them. Imagine their questions, their confusion, their amazement. Acts 2:43–47 describes their life together:

> Awe came upon everyone, because many wonders and signs were being done by the apostles. All who believed were together and had all things in common; they would sell their possessions and goods and distribute the proceeds to all, as any had need. Day by day, as they spent much time together in the temple, they broke bread at home and ate their food with glad and generous hearts, praising God and having the goodwill of all the people. And day by day the Lord added to their number those who were being saved.

It was a simple beginning for a group of people who slowly began to figure out how they would continue to make their way in the world in the absence of the One who had changed their lives. The description of this group is interesting. They were together, sharing what they had so no one was in need. They went to the temple, praised God, and gave thanks for the bread they shared around the table. Their hearts were described as glad, generous and full of goodwill.

When I think of how that scene is replicated today, I think of a congregation that gathers for Maundy evening meal and worship together during Holy Week. Tables are set with a soup tureen, a loaf of bread, and a chalice of juice. Families with children and teenagers come in and invite other church members to join them at a table. The remembrance of the last meal Jesus shared in an upper room with his disciples begins with the blessing of the meal.

After sharing soup, bread, and conversation, worship continues with reading the Scripture text for the day, prayers, and a meditation both on the text and on this day in Holy Week. Then the familiar words of the Lord's Supper are heard and Eucharist is shared around the table groups, as bread and cup are passed from a child to a parent, to a teenager to an adult. Those who wish are then invited to participate in another Upper Room ritual—foot washing. The evening concludes with prayer and singing, and God's people go out into the night.

There is something about this night celebrated in this way that connects with the description of the early Christians described in Acts 2. All are welcome. Parents are encouraged to come with their young children, because it is an experiential way to celebrate and remember. There is space to wiggle and move. Tables are simply yet beautifully set, and there is a feeling of welcome and hospitality. And then there is the meal shared among friends, two meals actually, the soup and bread and then the meal to which Jesus invites us.

The simple act of foot washing, a child washing a parent's feet, an adult toweling off the foot of a teenager—these are humble acts of sharing in community. "Day by day, as they spent much time together in the temple, they broke bread at home and ate their food with glad and generous hearts, praising God and having the goodwill of all the people."

In the section on the Holy Spirit, *A Declaration of Faith* describes the work of the Spirit in this way:

> The Spirit enables people to become believers.
> The Spirit enabled people of all races, classes and nations
> to accept the good news of what God had done in Christ,
> repent of their sins,
> and enter the community of faith.
> We testify that today this same Holy Spirit
> makes us able to respond in faith to the gospel
> and leads us into the Christian community.
> The Spirit brings us out of death into life,
> out of separation into fellowship.[2]

In both stories, biblical and contemporary, the work of God's Spirit is evident, leading God's people into community, into fellowship, from the various separated spaces occupied on a daily basis. To speak of spiritual fellowship of all God's children is to acknowledge this mysterious and ineffable part of the Trinity. We speak of God in terms of transcendence and immanence. God's incarnation in human form, Jesus, makes clear God's steadfast love of God's creation. And Jesus promises that when he leaves, the people whom God loves will not be left alone, will not be left comfortless, because God's Spirit will come and be present. The spirit binds us into being one body.

As the early church grew and struggled to discover how they could live together in community, they tried hard to understand and remember what they had learned from their teacher, Jesus. The letters in the New Testament provide insight about these struggles. In 1 Corinthians 12, Paul was concerned about how they were living together in the community and the ways in which the variety of their talents were being honored. "Now there are varieties of gifts, but the same Spirit; and there are varieties of services, but the same Lord; and there are varieties of activities, but it is the same God who activates all of them in everyone. To each is given the manifestation of the Spirit for the common good" (1 Cor. 12:4–7).

As the early Christian communities moved further away from the gathering described in Acts 2, they needed to be reminded of God's gifts to each person and how these gifts were manifested within the fellowship of Christian community. For Paul, the image of the body was a helpful analogy.

In writing about spiritual gifts, he reminded them: "For just as the body is one and has many members, and all the members of the body, though many, are one body, so it is with Christ. For in the one Spirit we were all baptized into one body—Jews or Greeks, slaves or free— and we were all made to drink of one Spirit" (1 Cor. 12:12–13).

In reflecting on the contemporary story of God's people coming together during Holy Week, I think about the gifts represented in this activity of spiritual fellowship. Some have the gift of making soup and baking wonderful bread for the Table. Others have the gift of setting welcoming tables with place settings and flowers. Some are given the gift of words for prayers and meditations, and others have the gift of welcoming those who arrive, making sure that all have places at the Table.

"God arranged the members in the body, each one of them as he chose" (1 Cor. 12:18). Some members of the body work the miracle of getting small children rested and dressed and present at the Table. Others have the gift of sharing bread and conversation with a three year old. And a teenager passes the bread to a member of his family and says, "This is the bread of life." Indeed, the body does not consist of one member, but of many.

In *A Brief Statement of Faith*, we acknowledge that trusting in God the Holy Spirit means that

> In a broken and fearful world
> the Spirit gives us courage
>> to pray without ceasing,
>> to witness among all peoples to Christ as Lord and Savior,
>> to unmask idolatries in Church and culture,
>> to hear the voices of peoples long silenced,
>> and to work with others for justice, freedom, and peace.

In gratitude to God, empowered by the Spirit,
    we strive to serve Christ in our daily tasks
      and to live holy and joyful lives,
    even as we watch for God's new heaven and new earth,
    praying, "Come, Lord Jesus!"[3]

Notice the way the Spirit is described as one who gives courage, one who empowers God's people to live thankfully in response to God's redeeming love, being actively present in a world described as broken and fearful. This statement was written by a work group of the PC(USA) in the late 1980s. How relevant still is this description of the world in the early years of the new millennium, a time when many of us experience it as even more broken and fearful than it was when this statement was written.

Considering this list of responsibilities is a bit daunting: praying, witnessing, unmasking idolatries, bringing to voice those who have been silenced, and working for justice, freedom, and peace. It becomes a bit more manageable when we remember that it is God's Spirit who gives us courage to do these things. It becomes a bit more manageable when we remember that we do these things together, in community, working with others, sharing our gifts.

This same Spirit who was present with the early Christians is present today wherever Christians gather in fellowship, giving and renewing life. As *A Brief Statement of Faith* reminds us, God's Spirit "binds us together with all believers in the one body of Christ, the Church." According to *A Declaration of Faith*, we come together not because we are good or perfect, or have all of life's questions answered. We come together because

The Spirit makes us aware of our sinfulness and need,
moves us to abandon our old way of life,
persuades us to trust in Christ and adopt his way.
In all these things we are responsible for our decisions.
But after we have trusted and repented
we recognize that the Spirit enabled us to hear and act.
It is not our faith but God's grace in Jesus Christ
that justifies us and reconciles us to God.
Yet it is only by faith that we accept God's grace
    and live by it.[4]

Challenging Possibilities

The last chapter suggested that what people most need today in the church is not Christian education but Christian formation, which includes education in and practice with spiritual disciplines that both shape and support Christian living. Spirituality is one way to talk about this life of faith. In writing about this topic, author Eugene Peterson has said that

> living fully and well is a goal at the heart of all serious spirituality. Spirit, in our three parent languages (Hebrew, Greek and Latin) carries the root meaning of breath and easily offers itself up as a metaphor for life. God lives and gives life. God lives and brims with life. God lives and permeates everything we see and hear and taste and touch, everything we experience.[5]

In response to this great gift of life, we say thank you.

According to Garrison Keillor, spiritual life begins in gratitude. When we lift up each of our blessings daily to God, we "will walk through those gates of thanksgiving and into the fields of joy."[6] For many adult Christians, Christian formation is concerned with worship, prayer, and perhaps reading the Bible. Being present at church on Sunday and working to live responsibly as a Christian in the world define the parameters of spiritual practices.

But the last decade has seen an incredible amount of research and writing on the topic of spirituality and spiritual practices, and the variety and form is much larger than prayer, worship, and reading the Bible. Dorothy Bass has written:

> Practices address fundamental human needs and conditions through concrete human acts. . . . [They have] practical purposes: to heal, to shape communities, to discern. . . . Practices are done together and over time. . . . Practices possess standards of excellence. When we see some of our ordinary activities as Christian practices, we come to perceive how our daily lives are all tangled up with the things God is doing in the world.[7]

When thinking about Christian practices, it is logical to consider those things in which individuals engage to nurture their life of faith: prayer, reading the Bible, and reflection on actions in light of the call to be Christian. Bass suggests there is a communal nature in "practicing the faith." When individuals make commitments in community to practicing the faith, then the faith of the individual and the body, the church, are strengthened.

In identifying a list of thirteen practices that he believes are consistent with the Reformed tradition, Craig Dykstra has said that

> these are the kinds of practices that the church's people engage in over and over again, because they are practices that constitute being the church, practices to which God calls us as Christians. They are, likewise, practices that place people in touch with God's redemptive activity, that put us where life in Christ may be made known, recognized, experienced, and participated in. They are means of grace, the human places in which and through which God's people come to faith and grow to maturity in the life of faith.[8]

Notice what Dykstra says about Christian practices and what they do:

- They place us in touch with God's redemptive activity.
- They are means of grace.
- They address fundamental human needs—to heal, to discern, to shape communities.
- They are ordinary activities that help us connect with God's activity in the world.
- They support and sustain our living faithfully in the world, helping us risk.

Dykstra's list of Christian practices includes these things:

- Worship
- Telling the Christian story
- Interpreting Scripture
- Prayer
- Confession of sin and reconciliation
- Encouraging others
- Being in service and witness
- Suffering with neighbors
- Providing hospitality and care

- Listening
- Struggling to understand the context of life
- Criticizing and resisting the powers of evil
- Working together to create social structures that sustain life in accord with God's will

When we look at this list, it is apparent how the communal and the individual are connected. Some or all of these practices are evident when the faith community gathers for worship or for some other fellowship activity. For example, observing the Sabbath as a priority of faith formation gives Christians of all ages the opportunity to grow in their experience with practices of faith. Considering this list, it is also remarkable how common and daily many of these things are that Dykstra identifies as a Christian practice—listening, providing hospitality and care, suffering with a neighbor, and encouraging a friend or family member.

The work of the Lily Endowment since the mid-1990s in support of research and writing in the area of Christian practices for adults, youth, and children has added greatly to our knowledge and understanding of how people grow in the life of the Christian faith. Many adult groups in the church are reading and studying the book edited by Dorothy Bass, *Practicing Our Faith* as well as the books that have been developed from its original chapters. Each chapter addresses an area that Bass believes is essential for spiritual formation: honoring the body, hospitality, household economics, saying yes and saying no, keeping Sabbath, testimony, discernment, shaping communities, forgiveness, healing, dying well, and singing our lives.

Following the publication of *Practicing Our Faith*, the Lily Endowment funded a study for teenagers. A book based on the study, *Way to Live: Christian Practices for Teens*, is being used in many churches as curriculum for Sunday morning services and evening discussion groups. Each chapter in the book was written by a youth–adult team, oftentimes a parent and a child. Practices identified in this book include living life, the Story, bodies, food, creation, creativity, work, play, time, truth, choices, friends, welcome, forgiveness, justice, grieving, music, prayer, and practice itself. A comment included in the book sums up one understanding of spiritual practices: "We're free to risk living in new ways because we live in the promise that God loves us even when we fail. Growing into a way to live is not like having to do our chores before you can have dessert. You can have dessert along the way."[9]

In the online leader's guide for *Way to Live*, the editors address inaccurate assumptions about Christian practices, pointing out they are NOT:

- add-ons to life—something we have to do in addition to homework or chores around the house. Rather, a practice is a "life-giving way of doing something that is already part of everybody's life in one way or another."[10]
- ways of showing God, ourselves, or other people how good we are. "God already loves us."
- rules or formulas to master—what is important is to discover which ones work for you in which situation.
- an invitation to be "spiritual but not religious." "Christian practices are rooted in religious communities, even though no particular community has exclusive claim on these practices."[11]
- based on required use of any code language or a secret agenda. Although written for teenagers, this list is also helpful for adults who may not have any spiritual practices as a part of their life.

The Lily Endowment has most recently focused on faith formation in children's ministry. Karen Marie Yust, professor at Christian Theological Seminary, has been leading the primary research in this area, and one issue that she has identified is that "moral values and safe spaces are more important to many parents than formation in faith."[12] Charles Foster has commented that "parents and church leaders no longer seem to be asking John Westerhoff's question, 'Will our children have faith?' but instead are wondering, 'Will our children be moral?'"[13]

Interviews with parents have led Yust to note that "many adults equate faithfulness primarily (perhaps even solely) with being moral." In response to her research, Yust has identified six themes she believes are essential in ministry with children in helping them claim faith as a gift of God. They are belonging, thanksgiving, giftedness, hospitality, understanding, and hope.[14]

A child's spiritual life has its foundation in the concept of **belonging**, as a child grows in her understanding that she is loved by God and by a community of faith. As a child grows, he learns to say please and **thank you**. Helping a child also learn how to pray, to say thank you to God is the beginning of a life lived in response to God's gifts to us and our world.

As a child grows, trying new things is essential for growth and development. Children have success and failure as they discover things they are good at, like building with blocks, putting puzzles together, drawing, dancing, or singing. When children's **gifts** and abilities are welcomed and encouraged, they grow up knowing they have an important place within their family and their church, places where their talents are welcomed and valued. A church that welcomes the gifts and talents of even its youngest members is modeling **hospitality**, and its children will learn that it takes the hands of everyone to make the world a place of peace, love, and justice for all.

Understanding the connection between who we are and how we live is essential for children and for everyone. Yust believes that taking the time with children to reflect on spiritual experiences is essential in supporting their growth in the life of the Christian faith.

The last theme Yust identifies in relation to children's spirituality is **hope**. Hope is "expecting that there is something more to human existence than what we presently see or know."[15] Children are full of hope and imagination, and adults can learn by spending time with them and listening. Nurturing hope in a child means we nurture their natural curiosities about the world and the mysteries of God.

The sacrament of baptism offers families the opportunity to reflect on their own life of faith. Parents who bring their children for baptism may wonder, "Will I be able to answer my child's faith questions? What Christian practices are necessary for me as a parent in order to be able to live with my child's questions as our family makes a commitment to faithful Christian living?"

It is essential that we surround parents with the support that will enable them to be faith educators with their children. The kind of environment that surrounds baptism is welcoming, holding, and believing. It is vital for parents to both practice and offer a faithful believing environment in the home, which connects to the welcoming, holding, and believing environment that we nurture and support in the life of the congregation.

A baptism is not complete without a question asked of the congregation:

> "**Do you**, as members of the church of Jesus Christ, promise to guide and nurture _____ by word and deed, with love and prayer, encouraging them to know and follow Christ and to be faithful members of his church?"[16]

Expressions of Hope

"Making a home for faith" is a concept I use to discuss the interaction between adults and children and the potential that is present for faith formation in our daily life. The impetus came from my reading and reflection and experiences of teaching and working with parents. It seems that time has become our most cautiously protected possession. Many harried and hassled parents, wanting the best for the children, the best that professionals can give, have, I believe, turned over the job of nurturing their child in a life of Christian faith to the professional, the church. I am hopeful that we can begin to reclaim the role for parents to be the primary faith educators of children.

In *The Cloister Walk*, Kathleen Norris wonders openly about how we "become exiled from the certainties of childhood. What happens to the creative and expressive theologians who are our children? Why do many of them often leave church at the first opportunity they have to make their own decision?" Writes Norris, "I wonder if children don't begin to reject both poetry and religion for similar reasons, because the way both are taught takes the life out of them. If we teach children when they're young to reject their epiphanies, then it's no wonder that we end up with so many adults who are mathematically, poetically, and theologically illiterate."[17]

Martin Marty has written that many participants in Christian education are "refugees, exiles, or rebels."

> I'm concerned about parents of children and youth who have exiled themselves from any responsibility for nurturing their child in the life of the Christian faith. I am concerned about adults who are refugees from faith, those who have rejected a tradition in which they were raised, and seem to be adrift in the culture with no theological moorings. I am concerned about the rebels, those who just don't fit in to "the way we do things here."[18]

If you ask adults what homemaking involves, you will probably hear a variety of answers. Whether the task is fixing a leaking roof or preparing a nutritious meal, most would agree that a lot of time, energy, and commitment is involved in making a home.

I have been spending time recently speaking with parents in local congregations about nurturing their child's faith. They seek information from me, and their requests often begin with a list of questions that "as the expert" I'm supposed to answer. They go like this:

- Why is there evil?
- Why does God let terrible things happen?
- Where is heaven? Is my dog there?

- From an eleven-year-old: Why isn't God doing the same miracles today as in Jesus' time, like talking directly to us? I know God is doing miracles in a different way today, not the direct approach. I would like it done both ways.

A way that I use to frame the questions from parents about authority, knowledge, and responsibility when they are making themselves at home with faith is to ask them these questions: If you can't solve the math problem what do you do? If you've forgotten what a simile or metaphor is, how do you help your child with their English assignment?

Parents are accustomed to sitting down and thinking with their child about school assignments, helping the child come up with his or her own responses. This same kind of parenting is needed with questions of faith and life. Just as parents are on a journey with their child to help him or her do his or her best work as a student in school, so too, they are on a journey of enabling their child to articulate his or her faith commitments.

Journey is a popular way to talk about the life of faith. As we move through life, our faith grows and evolves in new and mysterious ways. I like to use the concept of making a home for faith, which I think resonates with the intent of Deuteronomy 6:4–9. I use this concept not so much in opposition to the images of natural growth or journeys in faith but as an addition. Rather than conceiving of a life of faith in terms of a growing seed or a road, consider a home with windows and light, a door, rooms. This home is unique to each person, and so, some homes for faith can be found in tree houses or tents, apartments or grand mansions, cabins in the woods or balconies with window boxes near the train tracks. Making a home for faith is concerned with the intentionality of being aware of God and God's presence wherever you are.

I believe that some people, like those in the story that Sasso tells in *God in Between*, are so busy going on a pilgrimage looking for God, that they fail to recognize God's daily presence in their lives.

For faithful Jews, Sabbath begins in the home with *Shabbat* on Friday evening. Candles are lit, bread is shared, and prayers are spoken. This table celebration reminds Jewish families to sanctify time and to be aware of God's presence in their lives. From the table at home, they move to their synagogue for Friday evening services.

It is said about preachers that we preach what we most need to hear and hope that it also has some meaning for the hearer. I think that is also true of writers. It is not a coincidence that this topic of making a home for faith found me. Probably like a lot of you, I struggle to stay in tune with God, to have a rhythm of faith and life, liturgy and prayer, a way of living faithfully such as Dorothy Bass has described in her recent book as "receiving the day." She notes, "the practice of receiving the day is the cluster of activities that enable Christians to offer attention, daily, to the gracious presence and activity of God."[19]

Another educator, Dwayne Huebner, has spoken of receiving the day in terms of making a clearing for God in our lives. He believes this is an essential activity for parents because "the infant, in growing with a cluttered adult and without the necessary clearings for remembering, thanking, and seeking God, constructs or takes on idols, not clearings of faith. The structures of receptivity—of hearing, seeing, feeling—are cluttered and faithless, because the consciousness of the adult is cluttered and faithless."[20]

Receiving the day, making a clearing for God, promising to make a home for faith—these would be wonderful commitments to make at a child's baptism. What if we included some promises for the whole congregation to make. I will commit myself anew to learning the Christian story by living it and living it faithfully with children and youth.

A Catholic educator, Mark Searle, has said that being a faithful parent with children is more than teaching them what they (the parents) know. Searle has said what I have come to believe is true as I struggle with the realities of Christian education in the church school and the life of faith every day in between Sundays. "The story and the skills [of the Christian faith] are only partially conveyed in explicit lessons. Christianity, it has been said, is more caught than taught, and the model for learning it is closer to that of an apprenticeship than that of a classroom."[21]

Making a home for faith involves being and doing. Knowledge of the Christian faith is more than the ability to tell the story of Miriam saving the life of her brother Moses or of Mary and Martha preparing to welcome Jesus to their home. Knowledge is intimately connected with being faithful and having that evidenced in daily practice.

One of my favorite children's authors is Marc Gellman. He writes that the Bible "is kind of like a pair of glasses through which I look at the world. I see our stories in its stories. I see all of us in all of them, and most of all I see God there and see God here."[22]

I agree with the emphasis of Searle and Huebner on the intentionality required of parents in being faithful and living faithfully in the world. I also want to affirm the importance of the activity of knowing. To make use of the glasses that Gellman describes, one has to take them out of the case. A frame for being and doing in the world is enabled by the ability to be at home with the biblical story. Making a clearing for God and serving as a role model for a young apprentice in faith assume knowledge, understanding, and a wrestling with the biblical story in order to understand God's Word to us then, now, and in a future we cannot see or know.

From the variety of practices identified by Dykstra, Bass, and Yust it is apparent that nurturing the life of faith requires both communal and individual commitments. Spiritual fellowship within congregations is supported and sustained by practices of faith at home and in daily life.

Watching a television program on the ten things that children need to grow and thrive started me thinking about the things children need from faithful parents, families, and faith communities.

- Children need parents who are at home with their faith, who have practices of faith important for their own spirituality.
- Children need parents who help them make the connections between church school, worship, and the home.
- Children need caring adults who can interpret the life of Christian faith both in actions and in words and stories.
- Children grow in their own life of faith by participating with their family in the life of a congregation. They grow up knowing and experiencing Sabbath and the rhythms of the church year.
- In their involvement in the life of a congregation, children have the opportunity to learn and be with other faithful adults, teenagers, and children. Many families today live apart from extended family. For children to have a chance to be with other adults who welcome them in the life and work of their congregation is an important way of accomplishing this great end of the church.
- Children need time and space for their questions and wonderings about the mystery of God. They need faithful adults who are comfortable with their own faith, ones who can provide opportunities for children to explore through a variety of forms—music, art, drama, and biblical stories.
- Children today grow up in a world that is diverse in culture and faith traditions. Providing opportunities for them to have experiences of this diversity helps them understand and grow in their ability to live in this global family. Using the *Children's Mission Yearbook* at home and in the church is a great way to help children make these connections.
- Keeping and living the faith at home, following the liturgical calendar, and engaging in rituals of faith and learning are simple ways of having spiritual fellowship together.

- Children grow in their knowledge and understanding of the biblical story by having books to read and to be read from, especially Bible story books such as *The Pilgrim Book of Bible Stories* (Pilgrim Press, 2003, NRSV); *Bible Storybook* (American Bible Society, 1990, CEV); *The Family Story Bible*, Ralph Milton (Westminster/John Knox Press, 1996); *Augsburg Story Bible* (Augsburg, 1992); *Children's Illustrated Bible* (DK Publishing, 1994); *The Bible for Children* (Good Books, 2002).
- Children grow in their life of faith through families making time, being patient, and providing love.[23]

On the occasion of a child's baptism, parents and the community of faith are asked questions about their commitments to nurturing this child in the life of the Christian faith. To be able to model the living of a life of faith, adults need to identify some specific things they should be doing. Consider this as a beginning list of things we can expect of parents and other faithful adults in the congregation.

- can tell a Bible story
- can read a story from the Bible
- can deal with children's questions
- prays (privately and publicly)
- has time sometime during a day or a week for personal meditation, scripture reading, journaling, being with and listening for God
- asks faith questions—engages work, the newspaper, and the Christian faith
- struggles to understand and interpret affirmations of faith
- is a regular participant in adult religious education
- is a participant/lay leader in worship
- can explain the meaning of the sacraments and the liturgical year to a child[24]

Homemaking activities both "cultivate and shelter life," as Parks describes it. Preparation to live with a face of faith in the world requires that adult Christians make intentional commitments to nurturing their faith—both individually and communally. Establishing regular patterns of spiritual formation, habits of mind and heart, have the power to feed hungry souls and form a face of faith that can meet the world with all of its demands and challenges.

The connection Kathleen Norris makes between theological illiteracy and the ways we teach young children "to reject their epiphanies" is an important one. It is essential that our children learn the stories of faith, the liturgical words used in worship, hymns, and songs of faith. Equally important is to help parents understand that being with their children in affirming faith, living faith, and naming faith—the informal theological epiphanies that happen every day—teaches and empowers a life of faith in ways as effective and necessary as formal schooling in the church. Together, as partners, it is possible to raise children in faith so that their theological epiphanies are affirmed and nurtured.

Shaping Faith and Faithfulness

A helpful resource for this section of this great end of the church is *HungryHearts*, a publication of the PC(USA) that focuses on spiritual formation. In the spring issue, in 2004, the focus was on children and spirituality. In writing about this topic, educator Carol Wehrheim wrote this:

> As we think about children and spirituality, we are helped to remember that the natural curiosity and imagination of children plays an important part in their relationship with God. Being with a child can spark or renew our own curiosity and imagination, too often buried under layers of reality and years of disuse. Their questions regularly send us to deeper levels in our own thinking, and the best answer is often "What do you think?" Their fresh ideas push us to a new realization of the God who created and loves us.[25]

Participating in the life of a congregation, the place where all the children of God come together across the life span, provides a wonderful place to connect with the questions, affirmations, and curiosities of each person we meet there. In her article, Wehrheim provides a list of spiritual practices appropriate for children. Included in this list are:

- Praying: Prayers of thanksgiving, supplication, breath prayers, or the kind of prayers you can say in one breath; as well as listening for God in prayer, encouraging children to have silence at the end of their prayers so they learn both the habit of praying to God and listening for God
- Meditation: Teaching children and providing time for them to practice meditation, connecting with God or the biblical story through quiet reflection

- The Examen: This is an ancient practice of ending the day in reflection on consolations and desolations. When did you give God's love today? When did you give love to someone? When did you feel God's presence? When did you move away from God's presence? What are the sads and glads of this day?
- Music of the faith: Wehrheim writes that one congregation gives a recording of music sung by their children's choir to the family of a child being baptized.
- Stories of the faith and faithful: Reading and telling Bible stories
- Hospitality within the family and with the family: Providing opportunities for the family to do something together, such as prepare meals for someone in the church or for a homeless shelter. Children learn about this important spiritual practice by actually doing acts of welcoming others.
- Fasting: Wehrheim writes about how the spiritual discipline of fasting can focus on examining what you have and how you spend your time. Rather than watch television, a family might decide to invite a new member or family in the church for dinner and family game night.[26]
- Keeping Sabbath: Finding time to be family together

Spiritual fellowship includes all the ways that Christians are involved in the daily practices of their faith. In this chapter I have explored the concept of spiritual practices to provide encouragement and support for taking up something new, either as an individual or as a community of faith, or for making a renewed commitment to a familiar spiritual practice.

> In gratitude to God, empowered by the Spirit,
>> we strive to serve Christ in our daily tasks
>>> and to live holy and joyful lives,
>> even as we watch for God's new heaven and new earth,
>>> praying, "Come, Lord Jesus!"[27]

Notes

1. Anne Lamott, *Traveling Mercies: Some thoughts on Faith* (New York: Pantheon Books, 1999), 100.
2. *A Declaration of Faith*, chapter 5, section 3.
3. *A Brief Statement of Faith*, lines 58–76.
4. *A Declaration of Faith*, chapter 5, section 3.

5. Eugene Peterson, "Missing ingredient," *Christian Century* 120, no. 6 (March 22, 2003), 31.
6. Garrison Keillor, "Wobegon poets," *Christian Century* 120, no. 6 (March 22, 2003).
7. Dorothy C. Bass, *Practicing Our Faith: A Way of Life for a Searching People* (San Francisco: Jossey-Bass, 1997), 6–8.
8. Dykstra, 43.
9. Dorothy C. Bass and Don Richter, eds, *Way to Live: Christian Practices for Teens* (Nashville: Upper Room Books, 2002), 294.
10. *Way to Live*, Leader's Guide, www.waytolive.org, 3.
11. Ibid.
12. Karen Marie Yust, "Theology, Educational Theory and Children's Faith Formation." Findings for the Faith Formation in Children's Ministries Project. Unpublished paper presented at the Association of Professors and Researchers in Religious Education, November, 2002. Used with permission of the author.
13. Karen-Marie Yust, *Real Kids, Real Faith: Practices for Nurturing Children's Spiritual Lives* (San Francisco: Jossey-Bass, 2004), 19.
14. Ibid., 19.
15. Ibid.
16. *Book of Common Worship*, 406.
17. Kathleen Norris, *The Cloister Walk* (New York: Riverhead Books, 1996), 60.
18. Martin Marty, "Christian Education in a Pluralistic Culture," in *Rethinking Christian Education*, ed. David Schuller (St. Louis: Chalice Press, 1993), 22.
19. Dorothy C. Bass, *Receiving the Day: Christian Practices for Opening the Gift of Time* (San Francisco: Jossey-Bass, 2000), 19.
20. Dwayne Huebner, "Christian Growth in Faith," *Religious Education* 81, no. 4 (Fall 1986): 516.
21. Mark Searle, "Infant Baptism Reconsidered," in *Alternative Futures for Worship*, vol. 2, *Baptism and Confirmation* (Collegeville, MN: Liturgical Press, 1987): 48–49.
22. Marc Gellman, *God's Mailbox, More Stories about Stories in the Bible* (New York: Morrow Junior Books, 1996), xii.
23. Caldwell, 39–40.
24. Ibid.
25. Carol Wehrheim, "Children and Spirituality," *HungryHearts* (Spring 2004): 3.
26. Ibid., 7.
27. *A Brief Statement of Faith*, lines 72–76.

Questions for Reflection and Discussion

1. What place do you make for faith in your life?

2. How would you describe the home you make for faith?

3. What spiritual practices nurture and sustain your life of faith? How have these changed or evolved over your life?

4. If you have children at home, what are some of the faith practices that work for you?

5. What do you think it takes to make a home for faith?

6. What opportunities for spiritual fellowship in the congregation are important to you?

7. Discuss the two lists of things children need from faithful adults and the list of expectations of faithful adults. Which of the things on those lists are priorities for you? Which things are harder for you to do? Is there anything you would add to the list?

8. Review the list of spiritual practices identified by Carol Wehrheim. Which of these are ones that are important to you and your family? Which are ones you haven't tried?

9. Where in the life of your congregation are the issues that are raised in this chapter discussed or taught?

10. Compare the spiritual fellowship of the early church described in Acts and the spiritual fellowship of your congregation. What are the similarities and the differences?

Postscript

Blessings within the Nest

In 1997, the General Assembly of the PC(USA) focused on the great ends of the church in the services of worship. In her sermon on shelter, nurture, and spiritual fellowship of the children of God, the Rev. Linda Loving spoke about the nature of church by referring to the medieval mystic Julian of Norwich, who compared the church to a robin's nest "meant to protect the fledgling soul until it is ready to fly."[1]

Loving reminded the General Assembly that God's covenant that began centuries ago continues today.

> God's covenant promises that there is room for everyone in the nest, in the shelter of God's wings. We participate in the covenant by cultivating our churches to be not gothic fortresses, not social singles' clubs, not "drive-through communion," but fragile, open nests, where all who are needy and vulnerable and hungry for spiritual nurture and truth can gather for safety and feeding and friendship. Room for all, *all*, in the shelter of God's wings.[2]

The great end of the church discussed in this book urges the children of God across the life span to come together in the shelter of God's wings. Finding space and time together in the nest for nurture and spiritual formation become priorities for congregations who faithfully commit to living faithfully in response to this important mission of the church.

Coming together in the church, all of God's children become blessings to each other. In writing about confirmation as a blessing, Robert Browning and Roy Reed note the importance of adolescents having the blessing of their family and their congregation, the place in which their "faith is anchored and confirmed." They believe that "blessing is anchored in an understanding of the sacramental nature of all of life," life that knows no separation between the holy and the daily. "God is at the center of blessing but we are active participants in God's blessing as we become channels of God's Holy Spirit in our daily lives."[3]

I am struck by Browning and Reed's comment about how blessing is something of God, a gift bestowed by the creator on the creation. But at the same time in living in response to this gift of steadfast love, we become blessings to others as God's Spirit moves deeply in and through our lives.

Often in worship, the prayer of invocation before the reading of Scripture is this:

> Startle us, O God, with your truth and open our hearts and
> our minds to your wondrous love.
> Speak your word to us;
> silence in us any voice but your own
> and be with us now as we turn our attention,
> our minds and our hearts, to you,
> in Jesus Christ our Lord. Amen.[4]

Recently the Rev. John Buchanan began his sermon by commenting on this prayer.

> For many years I have begun my sermons with a little prayer: "Startle us, O God." Some of you like that prayer and tell me you miss it when I change it. Some have told me that they've been startled quite enough all week long, thank you very much, and the last thing they need on Sunday morning is to be startled again. I use that prayer for myself, if truth were told, because it is my experience that the capacity to be startled, surprised, astonished, can and does become diminished in us. We are so preoccupied, so focused on our goals, on our list of things to accomplish, people to see, calls to make, that we shut down whatever capacity we have for wonder and astonishment because it is a distraction from what we think is important.[5]

God's Word to God's people has always been a startling truth, one that creation has not always been ready to hear, to believe, or to accept. The shelter, nurture, and spiritual fellowship of all of God's children calls us to open our hearts and our minds to the startling truth of God's love, freely available to all. Yes, the nest, the church, is fragile yet strong enough to hold us all as a shelter. We are nurtured inside the nest by our life together, and we are supported and blessed for our mission in God's world as we grow ever more deeply in spiritual fellowship, being at home with our lives of faith.

May this statement of mission of the church provide you with the opportunity to take time for wonder, astonishment, for some startling moments as you consider the many ways you are called and blessed as God's child, one who lives in the shelter of God's wings.

Notes

1. J. Janda, *Julian: A Play Based on the Life of Julian of Norwich* (Boston: Seabury Press, 1984), 20.
2. Linda Carolyn Loving, "Bird's Nest or Hornet's Nest?" in *Birthing the Sermon: Women Preachers on Creative Process*, ed. Jana Childers (St. Louis: Chalice Press, 2001), 114.
3. Robert L. Browning and Roy A. Reed, *Models of Confirmation and Baptismal Affirmation: Liturgical and Educational Designs* (Birmingham: Religious Education Press, 1995), 66.
4. John M. Buchanan, prayer for illumination, Fourth Presbyterian Church, Chicago, February 27, 2005.
5. Ibid.